WORLD FAMOUS TREASURES LOST AND FOUND

WORLD FAMOUS TREASURES LOST AND FOUND

Vikas Khatri

PUSTAK MAHAL®

J-3/16 , Daryaganj, New Delhi-110002
☎ 23276539, 23272783, 23272784 • *Fax:* 011-23260518
E-mail: info@pustakmahal.com • *Website:* www.pustakmahal.com

Sales Centre

- 10-B, Netaji Subhash Marg, Daryaganj, New Delhi-110002
  ☎ 23268292, 23268293, 23279900 • *Fax:* 011-23280567
  E-mail: rapidexdelhi@indiatimes.com
- 6686, Khari Baoli, Delhi-110006
  ☎ 23944314, 23911979

Branches

Bengaluru: ☎ 080-22234025 • *Telefax:* 080-22240209
E-mail: pustak@airtelmail.in • pustak@sancharnet.in
Mumbai: ☎ 022-22010941, 022-22053387
E-mail: rapidex@bom5.vsnl.net.in
Patna: ☎ 0612-3294193 • *Telefax:* 0612-2302719
E-mail: rapidexptn@rediffmail.com
Hyderabad: *Telefax:* 040-24737290
E-mail: pustakmahalhyd@yahoo.co.in

ISBN 978-81-223-1274-4

Edition: 2012

Printed at : Param Offsetters, Okhla, New Delhi-110020

Introduction

Treasure-searching has been, through the ages, an extremely exciting and adventurous pursuit; it is highly demanding exercise calling for tremendous amount of courage and perseverance. Instances are many where those in pursuit of lost or hidden treasure spent long years – sometimes a span of as many as thirty years – in chasing their targets with single-minded devotion despite daunting and nerve-shattering hurdles in their way.

By and large, treasure-hunters have been motivated by either of the two objectives in undertaking their missions: the temptation to lay their hands on priceless gold, silver and jewels and go super rich in one knock; or to acquire precious knowledge about the civilisation, culture and lifestyle of the people in the olden times. Whatever be the aim, treasure-searching has motivated and will continue to motivate adventurers to plunge themselves into the realms of the unknown and mysterious.

In this book, you'll read more about world's great treasures which are lost and found, like:

- Nuestra Senora de Atocha – Discovered by Mel Fisher, the Atocha is probably the richest treasure ship ever discovered.
- Oak Island Treasure – The mysterious money pit, one of the longest running treasure hunts of all time. Does a fortune in gold lie at the bottom of the money pit? Proof that Shakespeares plays were written by someone else? Or maybe the money pit holds the treasure of the Knights Templar...
- Search for lost Biblical treasures like Ark of Covenant, Holy Grail, and Spear of Destiny.
- The Treasure of Cocos Island where mutineers hid the treasure of Lima on this tiny island in 1821. Was it really a notorious pirate haunt?
- The Kidd-Palmer Charts – Did a retired lawyer discover the secret of Captain William Kidd?

- Olivier Levasseur pirated Treasure on Mahé Island, Seychelles––Did a French pirate conceal a vast treasure in the Seychelles? Are the coded parchments he left as a treasure map authentic?
- The Royston Cave – A lost cave was rediscovered, when the people of Royston set about excavating the cave believing that a treasure was hidden within.
- The Lost Dutchman Gold Mine, probably the most famous lost mine in the world. With gold prices at record highs, whoever can separate the fact from the fiction and unravel the story of the Lost Dutchman Gold Mine will be rich beyond his/her wildest dreams.
- Hidden Hoards in the Mountains of Austria – Did the Nazis store large quantities of gold, silver and priceless works of art in hidden tunnel systems in the Austrian Mountains?
- Nazi Treasure in Lake Toplitz? Last resting place of the Amber Room? Millions of pounds worth of Nazi Counterfeit bank notes are known to lie in the depths of Lake Toplitz. Many believe that other Nazi treasures were dumped into the lake at the end of the war.
- Priam's Treasure – The Treasures of Troy discovered by Heinrich Schliemann. Priam's Treasure is believed to be in Russia, stolen in WWII by Soviet forces.
- Search for mysterious treasures of El Dorado and lost city of gold Quivira.

Contents

Famous Treasure Wrecks

Pirate Treasure – Hidden Plunder

Lost Mines, Caves and Tunnels

Treasure Maps, Codes and Ciphers

Nazi Gold – The Missing Spoils of War

The Search for Lost Legendary Treasures

The Search for Lost Biblical Treasures

Famous Treasure Wrecks

1 The Royal Charter Treasure Wreck

The Royal Charter was a steam clipper which was wrecked on the east coast of Anglesey on 26 October, 1859. The precise number of dead is uncertain as the passenger list was lost in the wreck, but about 459 lives were lost, the highest death toll of any shipwreck on the Welsh coast. It was the most prominent victim of about 200 ships wrecked by the Royal Charter Storm.

The Royal Charter was built at the Sandycroft Ironworks on the River Dee and was launched in 1857. She was a new type of ship, a 2719 ton steel-hulled steam clipper, built in the same way as a clipper ship but with auxiliary steam engines which could be used in the absence of suitable winds.

The ship was used on the route from Liverpool to Australia, mainly as a passenger ship although there was room for some cargo. There was room for up to 600 passengers, with luxury accommodation in the first class. She was considered a very fast ship, able to make the passage to Australia in under 60 days.

In late October, 1859, the Royal Charter was returning to Liverpool from Melbourne. Her complement of about 371 passengers (with a crew of about 112 and some other company employees) included many gold miners, some of whom had struck it rich at the diggings in Australia and were carrying large sums of gold about their persons. A consignment of gold was also being carried as cargo. As she reached the north-western tip of Anglesey on 25th October, the barometer was dropping and it was claimed later by some passengers, though not confirmed, that the master, Captain Thomas Taylor, was advised to put into Holyhead harbour for shelter. He decided to continue on to Liverpool, however.

Off Point Lynas, the Royal Charter tried to pick up the Liverpool pilot, but the wind had now risen to force 10 on the Beaufort scale and the rapidly rising sea made this impossible. During the night of 25th/26th October, the wind rose to force 12 'hurricane force' in what became known as the 'Royal Charter gale'. As the wind rose its direction changed from E to NE and then NNE, driving the ship towards the east coast of Anglesey. At 11 p.m. she anchored, but at 1.30 a.m. on the 26th the port anchor chain snapped, followed by the starboard chain an hour later. Despite cutting the masts to reduce the drag of the wind, the Royal Charter was driven inshore with the steam engines unable to make headway against the gale. The ship initially grounded on a sandbank, but in the early morning of the 26th, the rising tide drove her onto the rocks at a point just north of Moelfre on the eastern coast of Anglesey. Battered against the rocks by huge waves whipped up by winds of over 100 mph, she quickly broke up.

One member of the crew, Joseph Rogers, managed to swim ashore with a line, enabling a few people to be rescued, and a few others were able to struggle to shore through the surf. Most of the passengers and crew, a total of over 450 people, died. Many of them were killed by being dashed against the rocks by the waves rather than drowned. Others were said to have drowned, weighed down by the belts of gold they were wearing around their bodies. The survivors, 21 passengers and 18 crew members, were all men, with no women or children saved.

Royal Charter

A large quantity of gold was said to have been thrown up on the coasts near Moelfre, with some families becoming rich overnight. The gold bullion being carried as cargo was insured for £322,000, but the total value of the gold on the ship must have been much higher as many of the passengers had considerable sums in gold, either on their bodies or deposited in the ship's strong room.

Many of the bodies recovered from the sea were buried at Llanallgo churchyard nearby, where the graves and a memorial can still be seen. There is also a memorial on the cliff above the rocks where the ship struck.

Almost exactly a century later in October 1959 another ship, the Hindlea, struck the rocks in almost the same spot in another gale. This time there was a different outcome, with all the crew being saved by the Moelfre lifeboat.

The aftermath of the disaster is described by Charles Dickens in *The Uncommercial Traveller*. Dickens visited the scene and talked to the rector of Llanallgo, the Rev. Stephen Roose Hughes, whose exertions in finding and identifying the bodies probably led to his own premature death soon afterwards. Dickens gives a vivid illustration of the force of the gale:

"So tremendous had the force of the sea been when it broke the ship, that it had beaten one great ingot of gold, deep into a strong and heavy piece of her solid iron-work: in which also several loose sovereigns that the ingot had swept in before it, had been found, as firmly embedded as though the iron had been liquid when they were forced there."

The disaster had an effect on the development of the Meteorological Office as Captain Robert Fitz Roy, who was in charge of the office at the time, brought in the first gale warning service to prevent similar tragedies.

In recent years, the site of the wreck has been popular with divers. Much of the gold which was not washed ashore was in fact recovered by salvage divers in the months after the wreck, but many artefacts have been recovered in recent years.

Veteran diver Sydney Wignall recalls discovering a large gold bar on the site in the early days of scuba diving in his book, *In search of Spanish Treasure : A Diver's Story*. The bar was jammed solid in some iron work on the sea bed, he used his knife to try and free the bar. He found the saw edge of his knife cut through it very easily, but before he could cut all the way through his air supply ran out and he had to leave it, the flakes of metal stuck on the saw blade of his knife were essayed and found to be almost pure gold.

Before he could return to recover it, another storm hit the site and he was unable to relocate the gold bar. There is no record of this bar being recovered, so there is a very good chance it is still down there somewhere.

The remains of Royal Charter lie in very shallow water (8-10 feet), but the visibility at the site is usually very poor indeed. The wreck was smashed to pieces in the original storm and has broken up even more since.

Reports suggest that Australian gold sovereigns from the Royal Charter still occasionally turn up on the beach after major storms.

2 Dutch East India Company Ship Amsterdam's Silver

The Amsterdam, a ship belonging to the Dutch East India Company, was wrecked on the Bulverhythe shore near Hastings on 26 January, 1749. The ship was carrying around 2 tons of silver coins. The wreck site is protected under the Protection of Wrecks Act.

The Amsterdam was a 18th century cargo ship of the Dutch East India Company. The ship started its maiden voyage from Texel to Batavia on 8 January, 1749, but was wrecked in a storm on the North Sea on 26 January, 1749. The shipwreck was discovered in 1969 in the bay of Bulverhythe, United Kingdom, and is sometimes visible during low tides. The wreck site is protected under the Protection of Wrecks Act since 1974. Some of the findings from the site are in the Shipwreck and Coastal Heritage Centre in Hastings. A ship replica was built between 1985-1990 and can be visited in the Netherlands Maritime Museum in Amsterdam.

The Amsterdam was an East Indiaman or 'mirror return ship' (Dutch: spiegelretourschip) built for transport between the Dutch Republic and the settlements and strongholds of the Dutch East India Company in the East Indies. On an outward voyage these ships carried guns and bricks for the settlements and strongholds, and silver and golden coins to purchase Asian goods. On a return journey the ships carried the goods that were purchased, such as spices, fabrics, and china. In both ways the ships carried victuals, clothes, and tools for the sailors and soldiers on the ship. On an outward voyage of eight months, the ships were populated by around 240 men, and on a return journey by around 70.

The Amsterdam was built in the shipyard for the Amsterdam chamber of the Dutch East India Company in Amsterdam. The ship was made of the wood of oaks.

The maiden voyage of the Amsterdam was planned from the Dutch island Texel to the settlement Batavia in the East Indies. The ship, commanded by the 33-year-old captain Willem Klump, had 203 crew, 127 soldiers, and 5 passengers. The Amsterdam was laden with textiles, wine, stone ballast, cannon, paper, pens, pipes, domestic goods and

27 chests of silver guilder coins. The whole cargo would be worth several million euros in modern money.

On 15 November, 1748, the ship made its first attempt but returned on 19 November, 1748, due to an adverse wind. The ship made a second attempt on 21 November, 1748, which also failed and from which the ship returned on 6 December, 1748. The third attempt was made on 8 January, 1749. The Amsterdam had problems in the English Channel tacking into a strong westerly storm. For many days, she got no further than Beachy Head near Eastbourne. Black Death appeared amongst the crew and a mutiny broke out. Finally, the rudder broke off and the ship, helpless in a storm, grounded in the mud and sand in the bay of Bulverhythe on 26 January, 1749, 5 km to the west of Hastings.

She began to sink into the mud, where much of the keel remains today, perfectly preserved. Some of the cargo, including silver coinage, was removed for safekeeping by local authorities. There was some looting and English troops had to be called in to bring the situation to order. The crew were looked after locally before being returned to the Netherlands.

In 1969, the Amsterdam was discovered after being exposed by a low spring tide. It is the best-preserved VOC ship ever found. Archaeologist Peter Marsden did the first surveying of the wreck, and he advised further excavation. The wreck site was designated under the Protection of Wrecks Act on 5 February, 1974.

The Amsterdam

The VOC Ship Amsterdam Foundation started researching the wreck, followed by major excavations in 1984, 1985 and 1986, during which huge numbers of artefacts were found. Although the wreck is submerged in the sand and mud of the beach (and is even visible at very low tides), much of the excavation was done by divers, for whom a small tower was constructed near the wreck. Additionally, the wreck was surrounded by an iron girder frame. The archaeological output was so dense that new ways of researching needed to be developed, all of which were needed to understand the technological, socio-economic and cultural features of the VOC. Some of the finds are on show at the Shipwreck and Coastal Heritage Centre in Hastings, East Sussex, UK. The wreck is protected and diving on it or removing timbers or any artefacts is forbidden. The ship may be visited as the timbers are exposed at very low tides in the sand just opposite the footbridge over the railway line at Bulverhythe.

A ship replica was built in Iroko wood by 400 volunteers using tools of the period, between 1985 and 1990. It was floated to Amsterdam and is situated next to the Netherlands Maritime Museum (Nederlands Scheepvaartmuseum) where it can be visited. As for the original ship, there had been hopes in the 1980s that the Dutch Government, which still owns it, might excavate the whole wreck and return it for restoration and display in Amsterdam, like the Regalskeppet Vasa in Sweden, or the Mary Rose in Portsmouth, but the funds were not forthcoming. Several decks and much of the bowsprit lie submerged in the mud and are in remarkably good condition, being naturally preserved by the mud and much of the cargo is still aboard.

3 The 1715 Spanish Plate Fleet

On July 31st, 1715 a hurricane struck the Florida coast, sinking 10 of the 11 ships that made up the plate fleet of 1715. The plate fleets carried the Quinto, or royal fifth, a 20 per cent tax on gold, silver and other valuables traded in new world. The loss of the 1715 plate fleet was probably the largest loss of treasure at sea in all of maritime history.

The 1715 Spanish Gold

A beachcomber named Kip Wagner, a resident of Sebastian Creek on the Florida coast, walking the shore after a major storm discovered a coral-encrusted lump of coins, all dated 1714. After showing his find to another man, Kip Kelso, a search of library of congress was undertaken to see if more could be learned of the location of the wrecked fleet from contemporary documents.

At the library of congress, Kelso found a book called *A Concise Natural History of East and West Florida* by Bernard Romans. Written in 1775, only 60 years after the destruction of the plate fleet of 1715, Romans had visited Sebastian Creek and learned the exact location of the wrecked fleet from the natives who lived there:

'Opposite this river (Sebastian Creek), perished, the Admiral commanding the plate fleet of 1715, the rest of the fleet fourteen in number, between this and the bleach yard.'

Armed with this new information, Kip Wagner took to the sea on an inflatable tire inner tube and immediately found the 1715 fleet, their cannon laid bare by the same storm that had washed up the clump of coins he had found on the beach. After recruiting a team of divers (including a young Mel Fisher), salvage of the wrecks began in earnest, thousand of coins and artefacts worth countless millions of pounds were uncovered by Wagner's team. Salvage operations continue at the site to this very day.

The Controversial Treasure of Atocha

Nuestra Senora de Atocha (Our Lady of Atocha) was the most famous of a fleet of Spanish ships that had sunk in 1622 off the Florida Keys while carrying copper, silver, gold, tobacco, and indigo from Spanish ports at Cartagena, Colombia, Porto Bello in New Granada and Havana bound for Spain. The ship was named for the parish of Atocha in Madrid, Spain.

On September 4th, 1622, the Atocha was driven by a severe hurricane onto the coral reefs near the Marquesas Cays, about twenty miles west of Key West. With her hull savagely ripped open, the vessel quickly sank, drowning every one aboard except for five survivors (three sailors and two slaves). The Atocha was heavy-laden with gold, silver and precious gems, bound for the treasuries of Spain.

Impact of the Loss

After the surviving ships brought the news of the disaster back to Havana, Spanish authorities dispatched another five ships to salvage the Atocha and the Santa Margarita, which had run aground near where the Atocha sank. The Atocha had sunk in approximately 50 feet of water, making it difficult for divers to retrieve any of the cargo or guns from the ship. A second hurricane in October of that year made attempts at salvage even more difficult by burying or scattering the wreckage of the ship still further.

The loss of the 1622 fleet had an immediate impact on Spain, forcing it to borrow more to finance its role in the Thirty Years' War and to sell several galleons to raise funds. While their efforts over the next ten years to salvage the Santa Margarita were successful, the Spanish never relocated the Atocha.

Modern Recovery and Legal Battle

The cargo of the Atocha, valued at hundreds of millions of dollars by today's standards, lay lost beneath the sea for nearly 360 years. American treasure hunter Mel Fisher and a team of sub-contractors, funded by investors and others in a joint venture, searched the sea bed for the Atocha for over 20 years. The team discovered the wreck and associated silver, gold and emeralds in 1985. Fisher had earlier recovered the wrecked cargo of the Santa Margarita in 1980.

After the discovery, the United States government claimed title to the wreck, and the State of Florida seized many of the items Fisher had retrieved from his earliest salvage expeditions. After eight years of litigation, the U.S. Supreme Court ruled in favour of Fisher.

The mother load was finally discovered on July 20th, 1985. It was Mel's son, Kane, that radioed the news to Treasure Salvors head quarters on the Florida coast, from the salvage boat Dauntless.

La Nuestra Senora de la Concepcion struck the Los Abrojos reef, 60 miles north of Haiti after being severely damaged in a hurricane in 1659. Her cargo consisted of one hundred tons of silver and gold coin and bullion.

A survivor of wreck passed the location of the Concepcion's resting place to an Englishman named William Phips.

Phips, sponsored by King Charles II, set off to locate the wreck of the Concepcion in 1683. Arriving at Los Abrojos reef, he realised that he wasn't the only person searching for treasure, other ships were already there. Realising that his small ship and crew would be unable to fight off the other ships that had gathered in search of the treasure, Phips returned to England to try and secure a heavily armed war ship to escort him back to the Los Abrojos reef. He found several wealthy backers including the Duke of Albemarle who provided him with a total of three ships, two of which were heavily armed.

The three ships reached Haiti in 1686. One of the ships, the Henry, was sent to the search area immediately, the others stayed behind at Porto Plata. On the first day of the renewed search at the Los Abrojos reef, a member of the diving team paddling a canoe over the site spotted a strange looking sea plant amongst the coral below him, diving down to retrieve it, he saw several bronze canon. Search operations ended and salvage began. In

Mel Fisher with Atocha Treasure

the days that followed, the divers recovered thousands of silver coins and a number of silver bars.

The Henry returned to Porto Plata with the treasure and Phips ordered all three ships to the site to begin full scale salvage of the Concepcion's precious cargo.

When Phips eventually returned to England, he was carrying treasure worth £300,000. That's £300,000 in the money of 1687, it would be countless millions today. The bulk of the Concepcion's treasure was still on the sea bed, Phips had only managed to recover one third of the Concepcion's registered cargo.

Phip's primitive tools were not up to the challenge of cutting through the growth of coral that had covered the wreck site. Try as he might, he couldn't break into the Concepcion's Plate Room, where the vast majority of the silver was stored.

Ted Falcon-Barker

In 1967, Ted Falcon-Barker, an Australian treasure hunter and two companions arrived at the site to try their luck at locating the wreck and breaking into the Plate Room with modern explosives. They found 96 gold coins (all the coins were from the reign of Ferdinand & Elizabeth 1497-1516), a solid gold crucifix and a life-sized solid gold finger, possibly from a statue the Concepcion was believed to be carrying. The treasure hunt ultimately ended in disaster. Whilst on route to Port Royal for repairs to their boat and to pick up supplies, the crew dropped anchor over night in a small bay on the coast of Haiti where they were boarded by thieves. One of the crew, Hugh MacDonald, received a stab wound that would later prove fatal.

Falcon-Barker shot one of the boarders with a harpoon gun before firing on the rest of the would-be pirates with the shotgun he had onboard, but it was too late for poor Hugh, the damage was already done, the knife had punctured his lung and so far from proper medical care he didn't stand a chance. Falcon-Barker wrote a book about his attempts at salvaging the treasure of the Concepcion (*Devils Gold*, Nautical Publishing Company, 1969) which is well worth getting, if you can find it.

5 RMS Republic Treasure Salvage

RMS Republic was a steam-powered ocean liner built in 1903 by Harland and Wolff in Belfast, and was lost at sea in a collision six years later while sailing for the White Star Line. In her time, she was one of the largest, most modern and luxurious passenger vessels afloat.

History

White Star Acquisition

The ship was originally built in Belfast, Ireland for the International Mercantile Marine's Dominion Line (a sister company to the White Star Line) and was named "Columbus". After two voyages with Dominion, she was sold to White Star and renamed "Republic" (the White Star's original SS Republic of 1872 had been sold over a decade earlier).

Collision with Florida

In early morning of January 23, 1909, whilst sailing from New York City to Gibraltar and Mediterranean ports with 742 passengers and crew and Captain Inman Sealby in command, the Republic entered a thick fog off the island of Nantucket, Massachusetts. The steamer reduced speed and regularly signalled its presence by whistle. At 5:47 a.m., another whistle was heard and the Republic's engines were ordered to full reverse, and the helm put 'hard-a-port'. Out of the fog, the Lloyd Italiano liner Florida appeared and hit the Republic amidships, at about a right angle. Three passengers asleep in their cabins on the Republic were killed when Florida's bow sliced into her. On Florida, three crewmen were also killed when the bow was crushed back to a collision bulkhead.

The engine and boiler rooms on the Republic began to flood, and the ship listed. Captain Sealby led the crew in calmly organising the passengers on deck for evacuation. The Republic was equipped with the new Marconi wireless telegraph system, and became the first ship in history to issue a CQD distress signal. Florida came about to rescue the Republic's complement, and a nearby U.S. Coast Guard cutter responded to the distress signal as well. Passengers were distributed between the two ships, with Florida taking the bulk of them, but with 900 Italian immigrants already onboard, this left the ship dangerously overloaded.

RMS Republic

The White Star liner Baltic, commanded by Captain J.B. Ranson, also responded to the CQD call, but due to the persistent fog, it was not until the evening that Baltic was able to locate the drifting Republic. Once on-scene, the rescued passengers were transferred from the cutter and Florida to Baltic. Because of the damage to Florida, that ship's immigrant passengers were also transferred to Baltic, but a riot nearly broke out when they had to wait until first class Baltic passengers were transferred. Once everyone was onboard, Baltic sailed for New York.

Captain Sealby and a skeleton crew remained onboard the Republic to make an effort to save her. Crewmen from the cutter tried using collision mats to stem the flooding, but to no avail. By this time, the steamers New York and Lucania (from Cunard) had also arrived, and waited while an attempt was made by the cutter to take the Republic under tow. This effort, too was futile, and on January 24, the Republic sank. At 15,378 tons, she was the largest ship to have sunk up to that time. All the remaining crew were evacuated before she sank.

Rumoured Cargo

There are many rumours that the Republic was carrying gold and/or other valuables when she went down. One rumour is that she was carrying gold worth \$250,000-\$265,000 in American gold coins to be used as payroll for the U.S. Navy's Great White Fleet. Another theory is that she was carrying money for the relief effort for the 1908 earthquake in Messina, Italy. A third theory, put forward by Captain Martin Bayerle, is that she was carrying \$3,000,000 in gold coins as part of a loan to the Imperial Russian government. All of these values, of course, are in 1909 dollars when gold was \$20 per ounce. Today, the coin values would bring the recovery to at least many hundreds of millions of dollars, and some experts have estimated that the recovery (with proper marketing of the recovered coins) could approach $5 thousand million or more, making the Republic salvage the largest treasure recovery of all time.

Rediscovery

The wreck of the Republic was found by Captain Martin Bayerle in 1981. She lies upright approximately 50 miles south of Nantucket Island at Latitude 40° 26' N, Longitude 69° 46' W in approximately 270 feet of water. Despite numerous salvage expeditions, many ship and personal artefacts remain, and as yet none of the rumoured treasure has been found.

The Salvage Continues

In 2005, Captain Bayerle's exclusive salvage rights to the wreck were reconfirmed by the United States District Court, District of Massachusetts. He planned to re-survey the vessel in 2007, and was planning a major salvage for the summer of 2008. A 'section lift' of the vessel was planned.

The Vigo Bay Treasure Galleons

The naval Battle of Vigo Bay (or Battle of Rande) was fought on 23 October, 1702, (12 October in the Julian calendar then in use in England) during the war of the Spanish Succession at Vigo Bay in Galicia (Spain) between an Anglo-Dutch fleet commanded by Admiral Sir George Rooke, and a combined French and Spanish fleet commanded by Admirals François Louis Rousselet de Chateau-Renault and Manuel de Velasco.

Rooke had been sent with a large Anglo-Dutch force to capture Cádiz in Spain but retreated in defeat on 29 September, 1702. When the returning fleet put in to water at Lagos, Portugal, Rooke learned that the 1702 Spanish treasure fleet, one of the richest ever assembled, had sailed on 24 July from Havana, Cuba, and had been diverted from Cadiz to Vigo, where it had arrived on 23, September.

Determined to salvage something from the disaster at Cádiz, Rooke set out for Vigo, where he found that the treasure fleet was protected by a Franco-Spanish fleet of about 30 ships. Chateau-Renault had fortified the harbour by laying a boom of masts, covered by guns from forts in the town and on the island of San Simón, near the town of Redondela. On October 23, Rooke attacked, sending Admiral Thomas Hopsonn on the Torbay to break the boom, and landing the soldiers of the Duke of Ormonde to capture the forts.

The battle was a complete victory for Rooke: the forts were captured, Torbay broke through the boom, and all the Spanish and French ships were burned by their own side, run aground or captured. The French and Spanish suffered about 2,000 killed; the English and Dutch about 800. The victors recovered silver to the value of about £14,000, but a

Diving to find the treasure galleon in Tobermory Bay in 1909

The salvage steamer Breamer equipped with suction dredge, removing a sandbank from the supposed location of Florencia galleon in 1909

far larger sum – perhaps three million pounds – had been unloaded and taken away before the battle.

British guinea coins of 1703 bear the word VIGO to commemorate the battle.

Treasure hunters believe that some of the treasure may still lie at the bottom of the bay. This belief was incorporated into the plot of Jules Verne's novel *Twenty Thousand Leagues Under the Sea*, with Captain Nemo and his crew obtaining money by salvaging amongst the wrecks.

The Lutine Shipwreck

HMS Lutine was a frigate of the Royal Navy which sank in 1799. The Lutine Bell from the ship is preserved at Lloyd's of London.

Lutine was originally a French naval ship, launched at Toulon in 1779, with 26 guns. Her name is the feminine form of Lutin (translation: 'the tease' or 'tormentress' or more literally 'imp'). This was ten years before the French Revolution; on 18 December, 1793, she became one of the sixteen ships handed over to a British fleet under Vice Admiral Lord Hood at Toulon by French royalists. In 1795, she was rebuilt as a (fifth-rate) frigate with 38 guns. She served thereafter in the North Sea, blockading Amsterdam. She sank on 9 October, 1799, carrying a large cargo of gold, the majority of which remains unsalvaged.

Acquisition of the Lutine

On 27 September, 1793, the authorities in Toulon surrendered the city, naval dockyards, arsenal, and French Mediterranean fleet to a British fleet commanded by Lord Hood. The French vessels included:

"Seventeen ships of the line (one 120, one 80 and fifteen 74s), five frigates and eleven corvettes. In various stages of refitting in the New Basin were four ships of the line (one 120, one 80, and two 74s) and a frigate. Mainly in the Old Basin and, for the most part, awaiting middling or large repair, were eight ships of the line (one 80 and seven 74s), five frigates and two corvettes. The Lutine was one of the ships from the Old Basin."

During the siege of Toulon, the Lutine was converted to a bomb vessel, firing mortars at the besieging French artillery batteries (commanded by Napoleon Buonaparte). With the fall of Toulon on 19 December, the Lutine was commissioned into the Royal Navy.

Service in Northern Europe

The loss of the Lutine occurred during the Second Coalition of the French Revolutionary Wars, in which an Anglo-Russian army landed in the Batavian Republic (now the Netherlands), which had been occupied by the French since 1795. Admiral Duncan had heavily defeated the Dutch fleet in 1797 at the Battle of Camperdown and the remainder of the Dutch fleet was captured on August 30, 1799 by the Duke of York.

During this period the Lutine served as an escort, guiding transports in and out of the shoal waters around North Holland.

In October 1799, she was employed in carrying about £1,200,000 in bullion and coin from Yarmouth to Cuxhaven in order to provide Hamburg banks with funds in order to prevent a stock market crash and possibly also, for paying troops in North Holland. In the evening of October 9, 1799, during a heavy north-westerly gale, the ship under Captain Lancelot Skynner, having made unexpected leeway, was drawn by the tidal stream flowing into the Waddenzee, onto a sandbank off the island of Terschelling, near Texel. There, she became a total loss. All but one of her 240-odd passengers and crew perished in the breaking seas.

The loss was reported by Captain Portlock commander of the British squadron at Vlieland, who wrote to the Admiralty in London on October 10:

"Sir, it is with extreme pain that I have to state to you the melancholy fate of H.M.S. Lutine, which ship ran on to the outer bank of the Fly (an anglicisation of 'Vlie') Island passage on the night of the 9th inst. in a heavy gale of wind from the NNW, and I am much afraid the crew with the exception of one man, who was saved on a part of the wreck, have perished. This man, when taken up, was almost exhausted. He is at present tolerably recovered, and relates that the Lutine left Yarmouth Roads on the morning of the 9th inst. bound for the Texel, and that she had on board a considerable quantity of money."

H.M.S. Lutine leaving Yarmouth Roads, October 9, 1799, on her last voyage

"The wind blowing strong from the NNW, and the lee tide coming on, rendered it impossible with Schowts (probably schuits, local fishing vessels) or other boats to go out to aid her until daylight in the morning, and at that time nothing was to be seen but parts of the wreck."

"I shall use every endeavour to save what I can from the wreck, but from the situation she is lying in, I am afraid little will be recovered."

Three officers, including Captain Skynner, were apparently buried in the Vlieland churchyard, and around two hundred others were buried in a mass grave near the Brandaris lighthouse in Terschelling. No memorials mark these graves. A lake outside Terschelling is known today as the 'Doodemanskisten' (dead men's coffins), allegedly because it is also close to the place from which the wood for the coffins originated; an alternative explanation is that the name is a corruption of 'd'Earmeskisten', meaning a pauper's grave.

The failure of the gold to arrive precipitated the very crisis that it had been designed to prevent.

The Site of the Wreck

The site of the wreck, the Vlie, was notorious for its strong currents and the danger of storms forcing ships onto the shore. The area is composed of sandbanks and shoals, which the currents continuously shift, with channels through them: in 1666, during the Second Anglo-Dutch War, Admiral Holmes had managed to penetrate these shoals and start Holmes's Bonfire, surprising the Dutch who had considered the shoals impassable. The depth of water also constantly changes, and this has caused much of the difficulty in salvage attempts.

The Lutine was wrecked in a shallow channel called the IJzergat, which has now completely disappeared, between the islands of Vlieland and Terschelling. Immediately after the Lutine sank, the wreck began silting up, forcing an end to salvage attempts by 1804. By chance, it was discovered in 1857 that the wreck was again uncovered, but covered again in 1859. The wreck was probably partially uncovered between 1915 and 1916, although no salvage was attempted because of the war.

The Gold

The gold was insured by Lloyd's of London, which paid the claim in full. The underwriters, therefore, owned the gold under rights of abandonment and later authorised attempts to salvage it. However, because of the state of war, the Dutch also laid claim to it as booty.

Captain Portlock was instructed by the Admiralty on October 29 to try to recover the cargo for the benefit of the persons to whom it belongs; Lloyd's also sent agents to look over the wreck. The Committee for the Public Properties of Holland instructed the local Receivers of Wrecks to report on the wreck, and F.P. Robbé, the Receiver on Terschelling, was authorised in December to begin salvage operations. All three parties had drawn attention to the difficulty of salvage due to the unfavourable position of the wreck and lateness of the year. At this point, the wreck was lying in approximately 25 feet of water.

In 1821, Robbé's successor as Receiver at Terschelling, Pierre Eschauzier successfully petitioned King William I and by royal decree received the sole right to attempt the further salvage of the cargo of the English frigate, the Lutine, which foundered between Terrschelling and Vlieland in the year 1799, proceeding from London and bound for Hamburg, and having a very considerable capital on board, consisting of gold and silver coins, believed to amount in all to 20 million Dutch guilders. In return, the state would receive half of all recoveries. Eschauzier and his heirs, therefore, became the owners of the wreck by royal decree and thus are known as the 'Decretal Salvors'.

Eschauzier's attempts spurred Lloyd's to approach the British government to defend their rights to the wreck. In 1823, King William revised by subsequent decree the original decree: "Everything which had been reserved to the state from the cargo of the above-mentioned frigate was ceded to the King of Great Britain as a token of our friendly sentiments towards the Kingdom of Great Britain, and by no means out of a conviction of England's right to any part of the aforementioned cargo. This share was subsequently ceded back to Lloyd's."

The gold was apparently stored in flimsy casks bound with weak iron hoops and the silver in casks with wooden hoops. Within a year of the wreck, these casks had largely disintegrated, and the sea had started to scatter and cover the wreck.

Lloyd's records were destroyed by fire in 1838, and the actual amount of the gold lost is now unknown. In 1858, Lloyd's estimated the total value at £1,200,000, made up of both silver and gold. Despite extended operations, over £1,000,000 remains unsalvaged. An uncorroborated newspaper report in 1869 referred to the Dutch crown jewels being on board.

Initial Salvage Attempts

In August 1800, Robbé recovered a cask of seven gold bars, weighing 81lb. and a small chest containing 4,606 Spanish piastres. Over September 4-5, two small casks were recovered, one with its bottom stoved in, yielding twelve gold bars. There were also other, more minor, recoveries, making this year the most successful of all the salvage attempts; however, the expenses of the salvage were still greater than the recoveries by 3,241 guilders.

In 1801, although recoveries were made, conditions were unfavourable and the wreck was already silted up. By 1804, Robbé reported that the part of the wreck in which one is accustomed to find the precious metals has now been covered by a large piece of the side of the ship (which had previously been found hanging more or less at an angle), thus impeding the salvage work, which was otherwise possible. Salvage attempts appear to have been given up at this point.

In 1814, Pierre Eschauzier was allocated 300 guilders for salvage by the Dutch King and recovered 8 Louis d'or and 7 Spanish piastres fished out of the wreck of the Lutine.

In 1821, Eschauzier put together a syndicate with the intention of using a diving bell manned by amphibicque Englishmen. However, Mr. Rennie, the engineer, died that year; in 1822, the bell arrived at the end of June, but operations were frustrated by bad weather and silting-up of the wreck; at this stage the wreck was reckoned to be 3 feet under the sand. Although salvage attempts continued until 1829, little was gained and the bell was sold on to the Dutch navy. In 1835, the sandbank covering the Lutine shrunk and moved southwards, with the depth of water being 30-34 feet and further desultory attempts at salvage were made. Further attempts to raise capital were largely unsuccessful.

In 1857, it was discovered by chance that a channel had formed straight across the Goudplaat sandbank, leading over the wreck, so that the latter was not merely clear of sand but had also sunk further below the surface with the channel the bows and stern, together with the decks and sides, had come completely away, leaving only the keel with the keelson above it and some ribs attached to this. Recovery work immediately recommenced, now using helmeted divers (helmduikers) and bell divers (klokduikers), the latter using a bell called the Hollandsche Duiker (Dutch diver). However, a large number of unauthorised salvors also displayed an interest, which led Dutch government to station a gunboat in the area. Over the course of the season, approximately 20,000 guilders-worth of specie was recovered.

The 1858 season was hampered by poor weather but yielded 32 gold bars and 66 silver bars. In 1859, it became apparent that the treasure had been stored towards the stern of the ship, and that the stern was lying on its side, with the starbord side uppermost and the port side sunk into the sand. This area, however, only gave up 4 gold bars, 1 silver bar, and over 3,500 piastres. By 1860, the depth of the wreck had reached 45 feet and the quantity of salvage was declining. Nonetheless, over the four years, salvage worth half a million guilders had been recovered: 41 gold bars, 64 silver bars, and 15,350 various coins, and the syndicate paid a 136% return; attempts were finally ended in 1863 as the wreck again silted up.

In 1867, an inventor, Willem Hendrik ter Meulen, proposed using a 'zandboor' (sand drill), a device which forced water into the sandy sea bed in order to clear a way for a helmet diver and signed a three-year contract, subsequently extended for another three years and then a further twenty years. The plan was that when the depth of water reached 23 feet, the machine would be used to excavate the same depth of sand down onto the wreck. Ter Meulen bought a steel-hulled, paddlewheel-driven 50 h.p. steam tug, the Antagonist. The engine was modified such that it could be disconnected from the paddlewheels and used to drive the centrifugal 'whirlpool' pump. The pump was capable of pumping water at a rate of 28 cubic yards a minute, but tests showed that 2 cubic yards was sufficient, and the 'zandboor' took only a couple of minutes to penetrate through to the wreck. It was also found that the sand did not collapse once the diver descended through the drilled hole into the cavity excavated by the machine.

Unfortunately, the wreck remained heavily silted up, with the depth of water varying between a high of 6 feet (in 1873) to a low of 17 feet (in 1868 and again in 1884). However, ter Meulen was responsible for re-establishing the landmarks used for taking transits of the wreck site and for establishing its position: 53° 21' 33" 974 North, 5° 04' 41" 804 East.

Other Salvage

In 1886, a cannon was salvaged and presented by Lloyd's to Queen Victoria: it is now on display at Windsor Castle. Another was offered to the Corporation of London and is on display at the Guildhall, London. A final cannon was passed to the Lloyd's sports club in Essex. More are on display in Amsterdam's Stedelijk Museum, and at least four are in Terschelling.

The two bower anchors, carried at the ship's bow, each weighing 3.8 tons were recovered and put on display in Amsterdam in 1913. Consideration was given by Lloyd's to setting the anchors up as a monument behind the Royal Exchange in place of a statue to Sir Robert Peel, but this was not carried out and only the wooden stocks, marked Lutine, were forwarded to Lloyd's.

The Lloyd's Act, 1871

A brief history of the loss and salvage attempts is given in the preamble to the Lloyd's Act, 1871:

And whereas in or about the year 1799 a vessel of war of the Royal Navy, named the Lutine, was wrecked on the coast of Holland with a considerable amount of specie on board, insured by underwriters at Lloyd's, being members of the Society, and others, and Holland being then at war with this country the vessel and cargo were captured, and some years afterwards the King of the Netherlands authorised certain undertakers to attempt the further salvage of the cargo on the conditions (among others) that they should pay all expenses, and that one half of all that should be recovered should belong to them, and that the other half should go to the Government of the Netherlands, and subsequently the King of the Netherlands ceded to King George the Fourth on behalf of the Society of Lloyd's, the share in the cargo which had been so reserved to the Government of the Netherlands;

And whereas from time to time operations of salving from the wreck of the Lutine have been carried on, and a portion of the sum recovered, amounting to about twenty-five thousand pounds, is by virtue of the cession aforesaid in the custody or under the control of the Committee for managing the affairs of Lloyd's;

And whereas it is expedient that the operations of salving from the wreck of the Lutine be continued, and that provision be made for the application in that behalf, as far as may be requisite, of money that may hereafter be received from those operations, and for the application to public or other purposes of the aforesaid sum of twenty-five thousand pounds, and of the unclaimed residue of money to be hereafter received as aforesaid;

The ownership of the remaining gold is vested in half shares between the 'decretal salvors' and the Society of Lloyd's, Lloyd's ownership being governed under the terms of the Lloyd's Act, 1871, s.35.

Salvage Operations as to Wreck of Lutine

"The Society may from time to time do or join in doing all such lawful things as they think expedient with a view to further salving from the wreck of the Lutine, and hold, receive, and apply for that purpose so much of the money to be received by means of salving therefrom as they from time to time think fit, and the nett money produced thereby, and the said sum of twenty-five thousand pounds, shall be applied for purposes connected with shipping or marine insurance, according to a scheme to be prepared by the Society, and confirmed by Order of Her Majesty in Council, on the recommendation of the Board of Trade, after or subject to such public notice to claimants of any part of the money aforesaid to come in, and such investigation of claims, and any such barring of claims not made or not proved, and such reservation of rights (if any), as the Board of Trade think fit".

The Lutine Bell

The ship's bell (engraved 'ST. JEAN – 1779') was recovered on July 17, 1858. The bell was found entangled in the chains originally running from the ship's wheel to the rudder, and was originally left in this state before being separated and re-hung from the rostrum of the Underwriting Room at Lloyd's. It weighs 106 lb. and is 17.5 inches in diameter. It remains a mystery why the name on the bell does not correspond with that of the ship. The bell was traditionally struck when news of an overdue ship arrived – once for the loss of a ship (i.e. bad news), and twice for her return (i.e. good news). The bell was sounded to ensure that all brokers and underwriters were made aware of the news simultaneously. The bell has developed a crack and the traditional practice of ringing news has ended: the last time it was rung to tell of a lost ship was in 1979 and the last time it was rung to herald the return of an overdue ship was in 1989.

During the World War II, the Nazi radio propagandist Lord Haw-Haw asserted that the bell was being rung continuously because of allied shipping losses during the Battle of the Atlantic. In fact, the bell was rung once, with one ring, during the war, when the Bismarck was sunk.

It is now rung for ceremonial purposes to commemorate disasters such as the 9/11 disaster, the Asian Tsunami, and the London Bombings, and is always rung at the start and end of the two minutes silence on Armistice Day.

The bell has hung in four successive Lloyd's Underwriting Rooms:

• The Royal Exchange 1858-1928;

• Lloyd's building in Leadenhall Street 1928-1958;

• Lloyd's first Lime Street headquarters 1958-1986;

• The present Lloyd's building in Lime Street since 1986.

There is also a chair and table at Lloyd's made from the rudder of the frigate. The rudder was salvaged on September 18, 1858. This furniture was previously in the Lloyd's writing room and was used by the Chairman of Lloyd's at the Annual General Meeting of members, but is now kept in the Old Library of the Lloyd's building.

Pirate Treasure – Hidden Plunder

Oak Island Treasure – The Mysterious Money Pit

Oak Island (44°31′00″N, 64°17′57″W) is a 140 acre (570,000 m²) island in Lunenberg County on the south shore of Nova Scotia, Canada. The tree-covered island is one of about 360 small islands in Mahone Bay, and rises to a maximum of 35 feet (11 m) above sea level.

The Money Pit

Oak Island is noted as the location of the so-called Money Pit, a site of numerous excavations to recover treasure believed by many to be buried there. The island is privately owned and advance permission is required for any visitation.

Early History

Mid-19th century newspaper stories recount that in 1795, young Donald Daniel McInnis discovered a circular depression on the south eastern end of the island with an adjacent tree which had a tackle block on one of its overhanging branches. McInnis, with the help of friends John Smith and Anthony Vaughan, excavated the depression and discovered a layer of flagstones a few feet below. On the pit walls, there were visible markings from a pick. As they dug down they discovered layers of logs at about every ten feet (3 m). They abandoned the excavation at 30 feet (10 m).

About eight years later, according to the original nineteenth century article, another company examined what was to become known as the Money Pit. The Onslow Company sailed 300 nautical miles from central Nova Scotia near Truro to Oak Island with the goal of recovering what they believed to be secret treasure. They continued the excavation down to approximately 90 feet (27.43 m), and found layers of logs or 'marks' about every ten feet (3 m) and layers of charcoal, putty and coconut fibre at 40, 50 and 60 feet (12, 15 and 18 m).

According to one of the earliest written accounts, a newspaper article called 'The Oak Island Diggings' from the Liverpool Transcript (Oct 1862) at 80 or 90 feet (27 m), they recovered a large stone bearing an inscription of symbols. The pit subsequently flooded up to the 33 foot (10 m) level. Bailing did not reduce the water level and the excavation was abandoned.

Investors formed The Truro Company in 1849, which re-excavated the shaft back down to the 86 foot (26 m) level where it flooded again. They then drilled into the ground below the bottom of the shaft. According to the nineteenth century account, the drill or 'pod auger' passed through a spruce platform at 98 feet (30 m), a 12 inch head space, 22 inches (560 mm) of what was described as 'metal in pieces', 8 inches (200 mm) of oak, another 22 inches (560 mm) of metal, 4 inches (100 mm) of oak, another spruce layer, and finally into clay for 7 feet without striking anything else.

One account states that they recovered three small gold links of a chain from mud stuck to the drill. They attempted to prevent the pit from flooding by damming Smith's Cove, and later by excavating a shaft into what was believed to be a flood tunnel from the sea to block it and prevent the pit from filling with water.

The original 18th century story of the pit's discovery along with the mid-19th century newspaper accounts are based on unverified folklore and may be entirely false. The earliest published description of the Money Pit is a news article in the Liverpool Transcript newspaper in October, 1862. This included an oral account of the early years of excavation attempts as told by at least one digger. No supporting material or evidence has surfaced ever since and the story has been impossible to verify. Several researchers have noted that artefacts like the inscribed stone and gold chain links could have been placed in the pit during expensive excavation operations for the purpose of attracting more investors.

Documented History

The Money Pit was first mentioned in print by the Liverpool Transcript in October, 1856. More accounts followed in the Liverpool Transcript, the Novascotian newspaper and A History of Lunenburg County, but this last account was based on the earlier Liverpool Transcript articles and does not represent an independent source.

The next excavation attempt was made in 1861 by a new company called the Oak Island Association and apparently led to the collapse of the bottom of the shaft into a suspected void or booby trap underneath. The first fatality during excavations occurred when the boiler of a pumping engine burst. The company gave up when their funds were exhausted in 1864.

Further excavations were made in 1866, 1893, 1909, 1931, 1935, 1936, and 1959, none of which were successful. Another fatality occurred in 1887, when a worker fell to his death. Franklin Roosevelt (later President of the United States) was part of the Old Gold Salvage group of 1909 and kept up with news and developments for most of his life. About six people have been killed in accidents during various excavations.

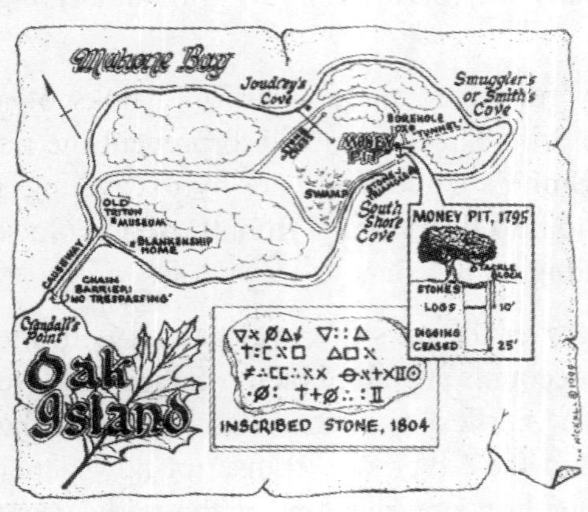

Oak Island Treasure Map

In 1928, a New York newspaper printed a feature story about the strange history of the island. Gilbert Hedden, operator of a steel fabricating concern, saw the article and was fascinated by the engineering problems in recovering the putative treasure. Hedden collected books and articles on the island, and made six trips there. Wholly convinced that there was buried treasure on Oak Island, Mr. Hedden even ventured to England to converse with Harold Tom Wilkins, the author of Captain Kidd and His Skeleton Island. Gilbert believed he had found a link between Oak Island and a mysterious map in Wilkins' book.

The very wealthy Hedden then bought the southeast end of the island. He did not start digging until the summer of 1935, following excavations by William Chappell in 1931. In 1939, he even informed King George VI of England about developments on Oak Island.

The 1931 excavations by William Chappell sank a 163 foot shaft 12x14 feet to the southwest of what they believed was the site of the 1897 shaft, close to the original pit. At 127 feet, a number of artefacts, including an axe, anchor fluke, and pick were found. The pick has been identified as a Cornish miner's poll pick. By this time, the entire area around the Money Pit was littered with the debris and refuse of numerous prior excavation attempts so it is unlikely the pick belonged to the original party (if any) that created the hole, however, that is not known with certainty.

In 1965, Robert Dunfield leased the island and, using a 70-ton digging crane with a clam bucket, dug out the pit area to a depth of 134 feet (41 m) and width of 100 feet (30 m). The removed soil was carefully inspected for artefacts. As a result, the location of the original shaft is no longer known by most, but not all researchers. Transportation of the crane to the island required the construction of a causeway (which still exists) from the western end of the island to Crandall's Point on the mainland two hundred metres away. However, four workers died during this attempt, when they were overcome by fumes in the tunnel.

Around 1967, Daniel C. Blankenship and David Tobias formed Triton Alliance, Ltd. and bought most of the island. In 1971, Triton workers excavated a 235 foot (72 m) shaft supported by a steel caisson to bedrock. Cameras lowered down the shaft into a cave below were said to have recorded the presence of some chests, human remains, wooden cribbing and tools, but the images were unclear and none of these claims have been confirmed. The shaft subsequently collapsed and the excavation was again abandoned. This shaft was later successfully re-dug to 181 feet, reaching bedrock; work was halted due to lack of funds and the collapse of the partnership.

The Money Pit Mystery was the subject of an episode of the television series 'In Search of...' which was first aired on January 18, 1979, bringing the legend of Oak Island to a wider audience. Previously, the story had only been known among locals, treasure hunting groups, and readers of sensational magazines and anthologies. The island has been loosely associated with the Freemasons and Templars, but none of this is proven.

During the 1990s, further exploration was stalled because of legal battles. As of 2005, a portion of the island was for sale with an estimated price tag of $7 million. A group called the Oak Island Tourism Society had hoped the Government of Canada would purchase the island, but a group of American businessmen in the drilling industry did so instead.

It was announced in April 2006 that partners from Michigan purchased a 50% stake in Oak Island Tours Inc., for an undisclosed amount of money. The shares were previously owned by David Tobias, and the remaining shares are owned by Dan Blankenship. Centre Road Developments, in conjunction with Allan Kostrzewa, a member of the 'Michigan Group', purchased Lot 25 from David Tobias for a reported $230,000 one year previously. Working closely with Dan Blankenship, the 'Michigan Group' has said they will resume operations on Oak Island in the hope of discovering buried treasure and the mystery of Oak Island.

Pit Flooding

Treasure hunters discovered coconut fibres beneath the surface of one beach called Smith's Cove (coconuts are not indigenous to Nova Scotia). This was discovered in 1850 and led to the theory that the beach had been converted into a giant 'sponge', feeding water from the ocean into the pit via a man-made tunnel.

Coconut fibres were also used as shipping dunnage and some say that the fibres may have been discarded from cargo ships stopping at the island or sailing nearby. The purpose of these fibres has been a source of heated debate among Oak Island researchers. But scientific analysis has confirmed it is indeed coconut fibre.

Oak Island lies on a glacial tumulus system and is underlain by a series of water-filled limestone cavities (Anhydrite) which could be responsible for the repeated flooding of the pit. Bedrock lies at a depth of 160-180 feet in the Money Pit area. However, bedrock does not come to the surface at that end of the island.

Upon the invitation of Boston-area businessman, David Mugar, a two-week survey was conducted by the Woods Hole Oceanographic Institution in 1995, one of many scientific studies conducted on the site. After running dye tests in the bore hole, they concluded that the flooding was caused by a natural interaction between the island's freshwater lens and tidal pressures in the underlying geology, refuting the idea of artificially constructed flood tunnels. Some scientists who viewed the videos taken in 1971 concluded that nothing of value could be determined from the murky images. However, other scientists confirmed that there were man made objects there.

Buried Treasure

There has been wide speculation about what the pit might contain. Most suggestions include treasure buried by either Captain Kidd, British troops during the American revolution, Spanish sailors from a wrecked galleon, the Inca or even exiled Knights Templar hiding the Holy Grail in the pit. A theory published by Penn Leary in his *The Oak Island Enigma: A History and Inquiry into the Origin of the Money Pit,* 1953, claims that English philosopher Francis Bacon used the pit to hide documents proving him to be the author of William Shakespeare's plays, a theory recently picked up on in the book *Organisten* (The Organ Player) by Norwegian Petter Amundsen and novelist Erlend Loe.

The notorious pirate Edward Teach (Blackbeard) claimed he buried his treasure where none but Satan and he could find it, leading to inevitable suggestions that he dug the pit, but there is no evidence to support this. The pit may contain nothing at all. Since the 1970s, fewer people have believed the pit has any connection to pirates, due to the massive scale of the subterranean structure.

The cipher stone (which disappeared from the island in 1919) has been translated many times with multiple decoders to read 'Forty feet bellow lies two million pounds.' Even this has been argued to be a hoax despite its appearing in nearly all early accounts of the island. The stone existed, but whether or not the often-noted decipher is correct remains in dispute. A cipher key and a coded message have been linked to Masonic vaults.

History or Legend

The story of the Money Pit is largely unverified and the gap of sixty years between the supposed discovery and the first known reports is very long. There is no surviving evidence that the nine platforms or 'marks' existed other than Vaughan's memories. Indeed, it is noteworthy that almost all of the debris, lost tools and other items mentioned in the early accounts have not been found. But a Multibeam Bathymetry survey by Bedford Institute of Oceanography of Dartmouth Nova Scotia in the mid-nineties indicates that there may be tailings off the eastern end of Oak Island. This speculation includes the two links from the gold chain, the inscribed stone, and even the tree itself. The piece of parchment does exist and is in the possession of Dan Blankenship along with a host of other objects.

Many elements contained in the Oak Island story, such as the discovery of tantalising but inconclusive objects and a message in indecipherable code, are common in fictional works on treasure and piracy (such as the Edgar Allan Poe story *The Gold Bug*). This has led many to conclude that the early account of the Money Pit is a romanticised combination of several works of nineteenth century fiction conflated with a local story about a search for buried treasure. It is interesting to note, all these popular stories came after the discovery of the Money Pit.

The Treasure of Cocos Island

The Cocos Island lies 350 miles west of Costa Rica which is tiny and uninhabited.

It is believed that a vast treasure was hidden here in 1821 by the mutinous crew of the Mary Dear (or Mary Deare, depending on source), a British ship chartered to move gold, silver and jewels from the churches of Lima, Peru to the safety of Spain.

Shortly after leaving the port of Callao, the gold hungry crew of the Mary Dear murdered the six soldiers charged with guarding the treasure, seized control of ship and sailed to Cocos Island where, it is said, they hid the treasure in a cave and then set sail for Panama.

Upon arriving in Panama, the mutineers were arrested, most of the crew were executed, but three were spared after promising the Spanish authorities that they would assist in the recovery of the treasure.

Two of the three were taken to Cocos by a detachment of soldiers, soon after arriving, the two men escaped from their captors into the dense jungle. The soldiers, unable to locate the mutineers and believing that the two men would be unable to escape the island, returned to Panama.

A year later, the two men were picked up by a passing ship and taken to Costa Rica.

One of the two passed on the location of the treasure, in the form of a map, to a man named John Keating. Keating, with the help of the third mutineer, a man named Boag, later located the treasure on the island but the crew of the ship that had taken them to Cocos demanded a share, facing a mutiny, Keating and Boag hid in the jungle until the crew gave up searching for them and sailed away.

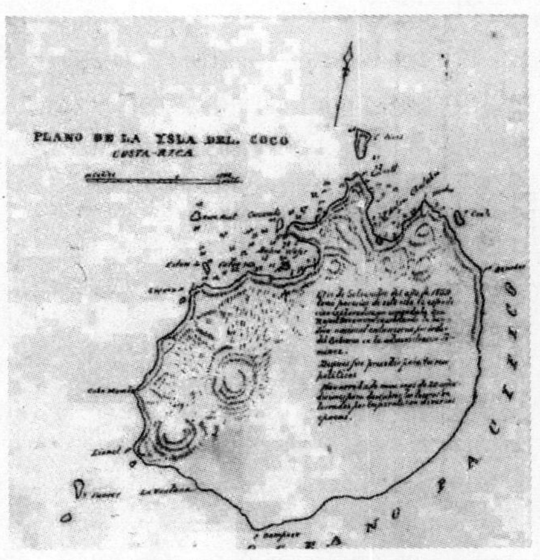

Cocos Island Treasure Map

After an unknown period, Keating was picked up from the island by a passing ship and claimed that Boag had drowned, although he would later say that he had murdered him and left his body in the cave with the treasure.

Before his death in 1882, Keating passed the Cocos secret on to three people (why he did not go back for the bulk of the treasure himself is not clear), his wife, Fred Hackett and Nicholas Fitzgerald.

Keating's widow and Fred Hackett teamed up and headed to Cocos – they found nothing. The third man, Nicholas Fitzgerald, did not go in search of the treasure but passed the map Keating had given him to Admiral Henry Palliser – who also found nothing.

It has been claimed that frequent earthquakes on the island have destroyed vital landmarks necessary to accurately interpret the clues on the map.

Many have gone in search of the Cocos Treasure, even members of Jacques Cousteau's crew made a somewhat half-hearted attempt at locating the treasure with a (now dated) underwater pulse induction metal detector during a visit to film the island and its reefs. (Cocos Islands: Sharks of Treasure Island, documentary film starring Jacques Cousteau and crew. From Cousteau's Rediscover the World series.)

Another notable to search for the treasure on Cocos was land and water speed record holder Sir Malcolm Campbell (father of Donald Campbell).

As far as we know, all who have searched for the treasure of Cocos Island have come back empty handed.

The Kidd-Palmer Charts

The Kidd-Palmer charts were discovered by retired lawyer and collector of pirate relics, Hubert Palmer, in a number of items of furniture that were said to have belonged to Captain William Kidd.

In 1929, Palmer bought a heavy 17th century oak bureau bearing the inscription 'Captain William Kidd, Adventure Galley 1669.' It is said that within the bureau Palmer found a secret compartment which contained a hand-drawn map of an unnamed island which bore the initials W. K., the words 'China Sea' and was dated 1669.

Palmer went on to track down two sea chests and a wooden box that were also supposed to have belonged to Kidd. Palmer claimed to have found further maps in all three of them, all depicting the same unknown island, but with varying levels of detail.

After Hubert Palmer's death, ownership of all four of the maps passed to his housekeeper, Elizabeth Dick, who took them to the British Museum to be examined by map expert R. A. Skelton. Skelton expressed the opinion that all of the maps were genuine 17th century charts, a fact that he confirmed to author Rupert Furneaux in 1965. (*Money Pit – The Mystery of Oak Island* by Rupert Furneaux, Fontana/Collins, 1976, page 43)

Elizabeth Dick sold all four maps in 1950 to an Englishman who later moved to Canada. Author Rupert Furneaux contacted the owner of the maps who told him 'The charts are fading badly.' (*Money Pit – The Mystery of Oak Island* by Rupert Furneaux, Fontana/Collins, 1976, page 43)

The current whereabouts of the four maps is unknown.

Hubert Palmer with Kidd's Map

Misdirection

Many believe that the island depicted in the maps is not in the 'China Sea' as the inscription claims, but is in fact Oak Island off the coast of Nova Scotia, Canada. The 'China Sea' inscription being a deliberate attempt to throw treasure hunters off the scent.

William Kidd and Gardiners Island

Some have noted that the island in the Kidd-Palmer charts does look a little like Gardiners Island (Suffolk County, New York State), where Kidd unquestionably did conceal goods and items of value in the Cherry Tree Field area of island in June 1699, shortly before his arrest for piracy. This treasure was recovered and returned to England by Governor Bellomont where it was used as evidence at Kidd's trial.

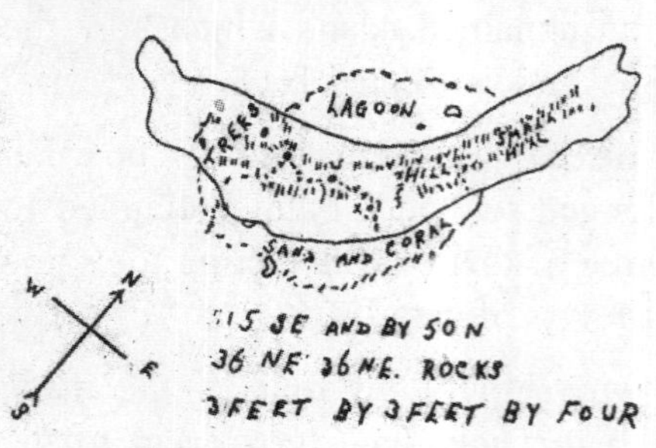

The Kidd-Palmer Charts

The recovered treasure consisted of gold and silver bars, gold dust (over 1000 troy ounces of gold and more than 2000 troy ounces of silver in total), rubies and other precious stones, silk, 57 bags of sugar and other more utilitarian objects. The treasure was sold off in November, 1704, for a total of £6437, the money used to found Greenwich hospital.

The location Kidd concealed the treasure on Gardiners Island is private property and not accessible without the landowner's permission.

Olivier Levasseur – Pirate Treasure on Mahé Island

Olivier Levasseur (1688 or 1690 – 7 July 1730), was a pirate, nicknamed, La Buse or La Bouche (The Buzzard) in his early days, called thus because of the speed and ruthlessness with which he always attacked his enemies.

History

Born at Calais during the Nine Years' War (1688–97) to a wealthy bourgeois family, he became a naval officer after receiving an excellent education. During the War of the Spanish Succession (1701–1714), he procured a Letter of Marque from King Louis XIV and became a privateer for the French crown. When the war ended he was ordered to return home with his ship, but instead of that he joined the Benjamin Hornigold pirate company in 1716. Levasseur proved himself a good leader and shipmate, although he already had a scar across one eye limiting his sight.

After a year of successful looting, the Hornigold party split, with Levasseur deciding to try his luck on the West African coast. In 1719, he operated together with Howell Davis and Thomas Cocklyn for a time. In 1720, they attacked the slaver port of Ouidah, on the coast of Benin, reducing the local fortress to ruins. Later that year, he was shipwrecked in the Mozambique Channel and stranded on the island of Anjouan, one of the Comores. His bad eye had become completely blind by now so he started wearing an eyepatch.

Olivier Levasseur

From 1721 onwards, he launched his raids from a base on the island of Sainte-Marie, just off the Madagascar coast, together with pirates John Taylor and Edward England. They first plundered the Laccadives, and sold the loot to Dutch traders for £75,000 (adjusted for inflation to 2008: £10,350,000). Levasseur and Taylor eventually got tired of England's Irish manners and marooned him on the island of Mauritius.

They then perpetrated one of piracy's greatest exploits: the capture of the Portuguese great galleon Nossa Senhora do Cabo (Our Lady of the Cape) or Virgem Do Cabo (The Virgin of the Cape), loaded full of treasures belonging to the Bishop of Goa, also called the Patriarch of the East Indies, and the Viceroy of Portugal, who were both on board returning home to Lisbon. The pirates were able to board the vessel without firing a single broadside, because the Cabo had been damaged in a storm, and to avoid capsizing the crew had dumped all of its 72 cannons overboard, then anchored off Réunion island to undergo repairs. (This incident would later be used by Robert Louis Stevenson in his novel "Treasure Island" where the galleon is referred to as The Viceroy of the Indies in the account given by the character Long John Silver).

The booty consisted of bars of gold and silver, dozens of boxes full of golden Guineas, diamonds, pearls, silk, art and religious objects from the Santa Catarina Cathedral in Goa, including the Flaming Cross of Goa made of pure gold, inlaid with diamonds, rubies and emeralds. It was so heavy, that it required 3 men to carry it over to Levasseur's ship. In fact, the treasure was so huge (estimated £100,000,000 in 1968), that the pirates did not bother to rob the people on board, something they normally always did.

When the loot was divided, each pirate received at least £50,000 golden Guineas (adjusted for inflation to 2008: £7,500,000), as well as 42 diamonds each. Levasseur and Taylor split the remaining gold, silver, and other objects, with Levasseur taking the golden cross.

Olivier Levasseur cryptography

In 1724, Levasseur sent a negotiator to the governor on the island of Bourbon (today Réunion), to discuss an amnesty that had been offered to all pirates in the Indian Ocean who would give up their practice. However, the French government wanted a large part of the stolen loot back, so Levasseur decided to avoid the amnesty and settled down in secret on the Seychelles archipelago. Eventually, he was captured near Fort Dauphin, Madagascar. He was then taken to Saint-Denis, Réunion and hanged for piracy at 5 p.m. on 7 July, 1730.

The Treasure

Legend tells that when he stood on the scaffold he had a necklace around his neck, containing a cryptogram of 17 lines, and threw this in the crowd while exclaiming: "Find my treasure, ye who may understand it!" What became of this necklace is unknown to this day. Many treasure hunters have since searched for his fabulous treasure.

In 1923 the widow of a certain Charles Savy named Rose found some carvings in the rocks at Bel Ombre beach near Beau Vallon on the island of Mahé, due to the low water level that year. She found carvings of a dog, snake, turtle, horse, fly, two joined hearts, a keyhole, a staring eye, a ballot box, a figure of a young woman's body, and the head of a man. A public notary in Victoria heard of this news, and understood those symbols must have been made by pirates. He searched in his archives, and found two possible connections. The first was a map of the Bel Ombre beach, published in Lissabon in 1735. It stated: "Owner of the land... la Buse" (Levasseur).

The second discovery was the last will from the pirate Bernardin Nageon de L'Estang, nicknamed le Butin, who died 70 years after Levasseur, and claimed to have gotten possession of some of Levasseur's treasure. It contained 3 cryptograms and 2 letters, one to his nephew:

> "I've lost a lot of documents during shipwreck.. I've already collected several treasures; but there are still four left. You will find them with the key to the combinations and the other papers."

and one to his brother:

> "Our captain got injured. He made sure I was a Freemason and then entrusted me with his papers and secrets before he died. Promise your oldest son will look for the treasure and fulfill my dream of rebuilding our house. The commander will hand over the documents, there are three."

The notary contacted Mrs. Savy, and after some excavations at the 'staring eye' they discovered two coffins containing the remains of two people, identified as pirates by the gold rings in their left ears, as well as a third body without a coffin, but no treasure was found at this location.

In 1947, Englishman Reginald Cruise-Wilkins, a neighbour of Mrs. Savy, studied the documents, but the cryptogram was much more difficult to solve than first believed. Deciphering it could be carried out only by starting from the two letters and the three cryptograms compiled in mysterious alphabet, a rebus, or at least in initiatory writing which could be put in relation to masonic symbolism. Cruise-Wilkins then discovered a connection with the Zodiac, the Clavicles of Solomon, and the Twelve Labours of Hercules. Various tasks, representing the Labours of Hercules, had to be undertaken in strict order. The treasure chamber is somewhere underground and must be approached carefully to avoid being flooded. It is protected by the tides, which requires damming to hold them back, and is to be approached from the north. Access is through a stairwell cut into the rocks, and tunnels leading under the beach.

Until his death at Réunion, Cruise-Wilkins sought and dug in the island of Mahé. In a cave, except for old guns, some coins, and pirate sarcophagi, he did not find anything. He died on 3 May, 1977 before he broke the last piece of code. His son, Seychello is history teacher, John is still seeking for the treasure, concluding that after using state-of-the-art equipment, he needs "to go back to the old method, getting into this guy's mind, claiming he is ten down, two to go in his Herculean Labours."

The Treasure of Loch Arkaig

The treasure of Loch Arkaig, sometimes known as the Jacobite Gold, was a large amount of specie provided by Spain to finance the Jacobite rising in Scotland in 1745, and rumoured still to be hidden at Loch Arkaig in Lochaber.

Background

In 1745, Prince Charles Edward Stuart (Bonnie Prince Charlie) arrived in Scotland from France and claimed the thrones of Scotland, England and Ireland, in the name of his father James Stuart (the Old Pretender). Although Charles asserted that his venture was supported by Louis XV of France, and that the arrival of French forces in Scotland was imminent, in truth France had little intention to intervene on the Stuarts' behalf. However, some limited financial support was supplied by both Spain and the Pope.

Spain pledged some 400,000 livres (or Louis d'Or) per month for the Jacobite cause. However, getting this money to the rebel army was the difficulty. The first instalment (sent via Charles' brother Henry who was resident in France) was dispatched in 1745. The French sloop Hazard (renamed the Prince Charles) successfully landed its monies on the west coast of Scotland. Unfortunately for the Jacobites, the riches were soon captured by Clan Mackay, who were loyal to King George II.

Lock Arkaig

The Treasure Arrives

In April 1746, the ships Mars and Bellona arrived in Scotland with 1,200,000 livres (another Spanish instalment, plus a large French supplement). However, on learning of the Jacobite defeat at the Battle of Culloden on 16 April, the ships left, unloading only the Spanish money at Loch nan Uamh, Arisaig on 30 April (the same place from where the Prince had disembarked the year before, and would later embark for France). Thus, seven caskets of Spanish gold arrived in Scotland. As the Jacobite cause was by then lost, with the army scattered and the Prince and his lieutenants in hiding, the money was to be used to assist the Jacobite clansmen (then being subjected to the brutalities of the government forces of the Duke of Cumberland) and to facilitate the escape of leading Jacobites to the continent.

Six caskets (one having been stolen by McDonald of Barrisdale's men) were brought to Loch Arkaig (just north of Fort William) and hidden. Their secret was entrusted to Murray of Broughton, one of the Jacobite fugitives. Murray began the distribution to clan chiefs, but when he was apprehended by the government (and later turned state's evidence) the treasure was entrusted first to Locheil, the chief of Clan Cameron, and then to Macpherson of Cluny, head of Clan Macpherson. Cluny was hiding in a cave at Ben Alder, which came to be known as "the cage", and when Charles briefly joined him there, Cluny had control of the money, which was still hidden at Arkaig.

The Treasure Hunt

Charles finally escaped Scotland in the French frigate L'Heureux, and arrived back in France in September, 1746. However, the fate of the money is not as clear. Cluny is believed to have retained control of it, and during his long years as a fugitive was at the centre of various futile plots to finance another uprising. Indeed he remained in hiding in his Highland "cage" for the next eight years. Meanwhile, a cash-strapped Charles was constantly looking for his money, and at least some of it came to him later, paying for the minting of a campaign medal in the 1750s. However, it is said that all of the gold was never recovered. Charles, years later, accused Cluny of embezzlement. Whatever the case, the gold became a source of discord and grievance among the surviving Jacobites.

In 1753, Dr Archibald Cameron – Locheil's brother, who was acting as secretary to the Old Pretender – was sent back to Scotland to locate the treasure. However, whilst staying secretly at Brenachyle by Loch Katrine, he was betrayed (apparently by the notorious "Pickle", a Hanoverian spy) and arrested. He was charged under the Act of Attainder for his part in the 1745-uprising and sentenced to death, being drawn and then hanged on 7 June, 1753, at Tyburn (the last Jacobite to be executed).

Dr. Archibald Cameron

The trail then goes cold. However, the Stuarts' papers (now in the possession of Queen Elizabeth II) record a host of claims, counter-claims and accusations among the Highland Chiefs and Jacobites in exile, as to the fate of the monies. The historian Andrew Lang (who was one of the first people to research the papers since Walter Scott secured them for the Crown) recorded, in his book *Pickle the Spy* (1897), the sordid tale, and the involvement of both the Prince and his father in trying to locate the monies. The Stuart papers also include an account from around 1750, drawn up in Rome by Archibald Cameron, which indicates that Cluny had not or could not account for all of it.

According to Clan Cameron records, some French gold coins were found buried in nearby woods in the 1850s.

Lost Mines, Caves and Tunnels

1 The Royston Cave – A Lost Cave Rediscovered

The Royston cave is a small but absorbingly interesting artificial cave in Royston in Hertfordshire, England. It was almost certainly used by the Knights Templar, who are also thought to have founded nearby Baldock. It is open to the public in the summer months.

Royston Cave is a circular, bell-shaped chamber 8 metres (26 feet) high and 5 metres (17 feet) in diameter with a circumferential octagonal podium. The origin of this chamber is unknown. This cave is unique in Britain – if not the world – for its numerous medieval carvings on the walls. They are mostly of pagan origin, but some of the figures are thought to be those of St. Catherine, St. Lawrence and St. Christopher.

It is speculated that it may have been used by the Knights Templar before their Proscription by Pope Clement V in the 1312. The sect held a weekly market at Royston between 1199 and 1254 and travelled there from their headquarters at Baldock, some 15 Kilometres to the southwest. They would have required a cool store for their produce and a chapel for their devotions, and a theory speculates that the cave was divided into two floors by a wooden floor. Two figures close together near the damaged section may be all that remains of a known Templar sign, two knights riding the same horse.

Royston Cave

Although the origin of the cave is unknown, the story of the rediscovery is very well known. In August 1742, a workman dug a hole in the Butter Market in order to get decent footings for a new bench for the patrons and traders. He discovered a buried millstone and dug around the curious stone to get the object out of the way. So he found a shaft leading downwards into the chalk.

At the discovery, the cavity was more than half-filled with earth. The rumour was that there must be a treasure buried beneath the soil inside the cave. Several cartloads of soil were removed, until bedrock was reached. The soil was discarded as worthless, it did not contain anything more than a few old bones and fragments of pottery. This is rather unfortunate, as today's archaeology could be able to solve some of the secrets of this place!

The location of the cave is also very interesting: Melbourn Street, once called Icknield Way or Via Icenia, was first used during the Iron Age, possibly 2000 years ago by an ancient tribe of Celts called the Iceni. The most famous Iceni was Queen Boudicca (died 60 AD). At a later date the Icknield way was Romanised by Caesar. It runs from near Falmouth towards East Anglia – the modern day A505 between Royston and Baldock, follows the route of the Icknield way, until it meets the Royston Bypass.

Today, the entrance is not by the original opening, but by a passage dug in 1790 and it is still possible to appreciate the sculptures which are almost as good today as when they were completed, possibly 800 years ago.

It is thought that the sculptures were originally coloured, but little trace of this is visible now. For the most part, they represent scenes of religious significance, amongst them the Crucifixion and various saints. St Lawrence is depicted holding the grid iron on which he was martyred. A crowned figure holding a wheel is thought to be St Catherine and large figure with a staff and a child on his shoulder represents St Christopher. A figure with a drawn sword is thought to be St Michael or possibly St George. Another possibly religious symbol is the depiction of a naked woman known as a Sheela Na Gig. This figure is normally found on 11th-13th century churches so its inclusion with religious symbolism is not out of place.

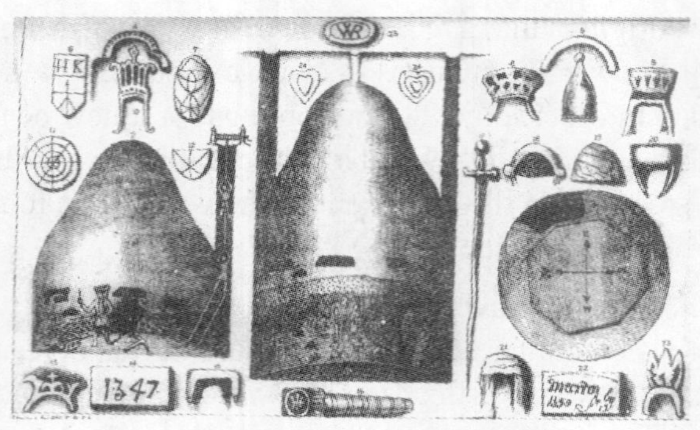

Royston Cave Treasure

The fact that these sculptures are of uncertain antiquity adds to their interest and offers visitors a chance to speculate on their origins. There are number holes, sometimes directly beneath the sculptures, which were thought to hold candles or lamps which would have illuminated the carvings.

Some theories suggest the cave may originally have been a Neolithic flint mine.

Lasseter's Reef Treasure

Lasseter's Reef refers to the purported discovery, in 1897, of a fabulously rich gold deposit in a remote and desolate corner of central Australia. The gold reef's location remains a mystery – if it exists.

Discovery

In 1929 and 1930, Harold Bell Lasseter claimed that in 1897, as a young man, he rode on horse from Queensland to the West Australian goldfields, during which he stumbled across a huge gold reef somewhere near the border between the Northern Territory and Western Australia. He also claimed that subsequent to this discovery he got into difficulties and was fortuitously rescued by a passing Afghan camel driver who took him to the camp of a surveyor named Harding. Harding and Lasseter were said to have later returned to the reef in the attempt to fix its location, but failed because their watches were inaccurate.

According to Lasseter, he spent the next three decades trying to raise sufficient interest to fund an expedition into the interior. But at the time the fortunes being made from the gold rush at Kalgoorlie in Western Australia meant that no one was prepared to risk trekking into the uncharted desert wilderness of central Australia, even if the supposed discovery was as rich as he claimed.

The 1930 Expedition

By 1930, when Australia was in the grip of the Great Depression, the attractions of desert gold were much greater, and Lasseter succeeded in securing approximately £50,000 in private funding towards an expedition to relocate the reef. Unusual for the time, this expedition included motorised vehicular transport and an aircraft. Accompanying Lasseter were experienced bushmen Fred Blakeley and Fred Colson as well as a prospector, an engineer, an explorer and a pilot.

Once they hit the trail, Lasseter proved to be a sullen companion and a vague guide. The group endured great logistical difficulties and physical hardships (including the loss of their plane), and on reaching Mount Marjorie (now Mount Leisler), Lasseter declared that they were, in fact, 150 miles too far north of the search zone. Exasperated, Blakeley declared Lasseter a charlatan, and decided to end the expedition. The expedition parted with Lasseter at Ilbilba; however, Lasseter insisted on continuing the trek. Accompanied by a dingo-shooter named Paul Johns, Lasseter, whose behaviour was later reported as becoming increasingly erratic, set off towards the Olgas.

One afternoon, Lasseter returned to camp with some concealed rock samples and announced that he had relocated the gold reef. He refused, however, to reveal its location. Johns, who by now doubted Lasseter's sanity, accused him of being a liar. A fight ensued, and Johns left Lasseter to his own devices, returning to 'civilisation'. Lasseter himself trudged off into the desert sands.

A search for Lasseter was conducted subsequently by a bushman named Bob Buck. Buck succeeded in finding Lasseter's emaciated body at Winter's Glen and, some way away, some personal effects in a cave at Hull's Creek. It later emerged from a "diary" which Buck found buried inside the cave, that after Johns had left, Lasseter's camels bolted, leaving him alone in the desert without any means of sustaining himself or returning home. He had then encountered a group of nomadic Aborigines, who rendered him what assistance they could with food and shelter; but a weakened and blinded Lasseter eventually succumbed to malnutrition and exhaustion, having made a belated attempt to walk from the cave to Ayers Rock or the Olgas.

Lasseter Reaf Treasure

Later History

No maps showing the location of the fabled gold reef were ever found, and over subsequent decades the tale of the reef and its discoverer has assumed mythic proportions; it is perhaps the most famous lost mine legend in Australia, and remains a "holy grail" among Australian prospectors. Popular adventure-story author Ion Idriess, in his book

'*Lasseter's Last Ride*', gives a very detailed description of Lasseter's time with the Aborigines. His 'diary' notes were hidden under campfires to hide them from the Aborigines who tired of Lasseter after their 'witchdoctor' pointed the bone at him. Once that happened, he was condemned to die and was no longer cared for by the tribe, whose members refused him food and water.

The Lost Tunnel of Leechtown

Some time in the 1950's, a gold prospector named Ed Mullard made a startling discovery near the deserted gold rush town of Leechtown, on Vancouver Island, about 25 miles from Victoria.

One evening, when Ed Mullard was hunting deer, forcing his way through waist-high vegetation, he suddenly found himself descending a staircase hewn from the mountain rock and facing an oblong or arched (depending on source) entrance into a sheer cliff face. Descending the stairs and entering the tunnel, he found himself in a long man-made gallery carved from the solid rock.

At the end of the gallery was another large carved arch that Mullard reportedly likened to those that you might see in a church. Moving further into the gallery, Mullard saw that beyond the arch were more steps descending into another large man-made gallery. Walking down the steps into the second gallery, Mullard found himself ankle-deep in water, but by match-light could see another arch and a third gallery through the gloom in front of him.

Mullard reportedly claimed that chisel marks were still clearly visible on the steps and the arches, and also that they were clearly of great age.

Sources differ considerably on what happened next (in fact, sources differ on just about every aspect of this story, as is the case with all great treasure mysteries), some say that while exploring the man-made galleries he found:

- Tools, weapons and artefacts that might have been Spanish in origin, or
- That he found one or more gold ingots, or
- That the things he found inside – tools and pottery – were unquestionably Chinese in origin.

Some say he found nothing at all.

After leaving the tunnel, Ed memorised its location and returned to his camp. Knowing that he may have difficulty locating his discovery again he left a trail of marks on trees (said to be his initials, 'EM') to help him relocate the tunnel entrance amongst the thick foliage.

Leechtown

Once he returned to civilisation, he told the tale of the mystery tunnel to many people, but he did not reveal its exact location to anybody. The Colonist newspaper agreed to fund an expedition to return to the tunnel in 1959, Mullard said he would be happy to lead the members of the party to the tunnel, but he died before the expedition had taken place, taking the exact location of the tunnel to his grave.

Despite several attempts to locate the Lost Tunnel of Leechtown, it has never been seen since the fateful day that Ed Mullard stumbled across it.

Leechtown, Jordan Meadows and Victoria Folklore

Vancouver Island certainly seems to be rich in folklore, particularly legends about an early Spanish occupation of the island. Here are a few more bits of local folklore possibly connected to the lost tunnel:

Jordan Meadows is reputedly home to a mystery bronze cannon (some sources say a Spanish bronze cannon) that has apparently been seen many times by hunters and prospectors travelling through the area, none of whom were ever able to relocate it when they wanted to show it to somebody or attempt to salvage it.

A legend very similar to the above cannon story is the bronze tablet or plaque that has supposedly been seen in the same area many times, attached to, or though growth became part of, a tree. Again, it seems that those who see this bronze tablet or plaque are never able to relocate it.

Rumours that a Spanish monastery existed in the area have reportedly persisted for many years. Some have linked the tunnel to the monastery legend; that the tunnel may have been the monastery (or, at very least, a part of it), or that those that built the rumoured monastery were also responsible for carving the tunnel. However, I have not heard of any hard evidence to support the existence of an early Spanish monastery anywhere on Vancouver Island, but it has been reported that Spanish artefacts have been found in the area.

Rumours that a gold prospector working in the Leechtown or Jordan Meadows area found some Spanish swords and armour.

Cannon Wreck off Vancouver Island

Sightings of a cannon wreck have been reported off the southern coast of Vancouver Island.

The Lost Dutchman Gold Mine

The Lost Dutchman Gold Mine (also known by many similar names) is reportedly a very rich gold mine hidden in the Superstition Mountains, near Apache Junction, east of Phoenix, Arizona in the United States. The land is a designated Wilderness Area, and mining is now restricted there by Title 16, chapter 23 paragraph 1133 of the United States Code.

The mine is named after German immigrant Jacob Waltz ("Dutchman" was a common, though inaccurate, American slang term for "German," derived from the German word for "German" – "Deutsch"). It is perhaps the most famous lost mine in American history: Arizona place-name expert Byrd Granger notes that, as of 1977, the Lost Dutchman story was printed or cited at least six times more often than two other fairly well-known tales, the story of Captain Kidd's lost treasure, and the story of the Lost Pegleg mine in California. Robert Blair notes that people have been seeking the Lost Dutchman mine since at least 1892, while Granger writes that according to one estimate, 8,000 people annually made some effort to locate the Lost Dutchman's mine. Former Arizona Attorney General Bob Corbin is among those who have looked for the mine. Others have argued the mine has little or no basis in fact and is a legend though, as noted below, Blair argues that all the main components of the story have at least some basis in fact.

According to many versions of the tale, the mine is either cursed, or protected by enigmatic guardians who wish to keep the mine's location a secret.

Other Lost Dutchman Mines

Blair writes that there have been at least four legendary Lost Dutchman gold mines in the American West, including the famed Superstition mine of Jacob Waltz. One Lost Dutchman mine is said to be in Colorado, another in California; two are said to be

Lost Dutchman State Park

located in Arizona. Tales of these other Lost Dutchman mines can be traced to at least in the 1870s. The earliest Lost Dutchman mine in Arizona was said to have been near Wickenburg, about 180 km (110 mi) north-west of the Superstition Mountains: a "Dutchman" was allegedly discovered dead in the desert near Wickenburg in the 1870s alongside saddlebags filled with gold. Blair suggests that "fragments of this legend have perhaps become attached to the mythical mine of Jacob Waltz". What would seem to be a crucial detail is also in dispute, as some allege that the so-called "mine" is actually a mine in the Superstition Mountains, or is instead a hidden stockpile of gold ore and/or bullion and/or coins.

Stories about the Mine

John D Wilburn in his book, *Dutchman's Lost Ledge of Gold*, 1990, points out that the Bulldog Gold Mine near Goldfield, Arizona, fits very well the description Jacob Waltz gave as the location of his 'lost mine'. He states that geology indicates that there is no gold in the Superstition Mountains, which are igneous in origin.

Granger writes that "fact and fiction blend in the tales", but that there are three main elements to the story:

"They are, first, tales of the lost Apache gold or Dr. Thorne's mine; second, tales about the Lost Dutchman; and, third, stories of the soldiers' lost gold vein ... the most complete version of the Lost Dutchman story incorporates all three legends". As noted, Blair argues that there are kernels of truth at the heart of each of these three main stories, though the popular story is often badly garbled from the actual account.

In 1977, Granger identified 62 variants of the Lost Dutchman story – some of the variations are minor, but others are substantial, casting the story in a very different light from the other versions. Keeping in mind that there are sometimes considerable variance between the tales, below is a brief summary of each of the three stories identified by Granger.

Lost Apache Gold, or Dr. Thorne's Story

In this story (actually two interconnected stories), members of the Apache tribe are said to have a very rich gold mine located in the

Superstition Mountains. Famed Apache Geronimo is sometimes mentioned in relation to this story. In most variants of the story, the family of a man called Miguel Peralta discovered the mine and began mining the gold there, only to be attacked or massacred by Apaches in about 1850 in the supposed Peralta massacre. Years later, a man called Dr. Thorne treats an ailing or wounded Apache (often alleged to be a chieftain) and is rewarded with a trip to a rich gold mine. He is blindfolded and taken there by a circuitous route, and is allowed to take as much gold ore as he can carry before again being escorted blindfolded from the site by the Apaches. Thorne is said to be either unwilling or unable to relocate the mine.

Lost Dutchman Caves and Mines

The Truth about the Peralta Mine

Blair insists that the Peralta portion of the story is unreliable, writing: "The operation of a gold mine in the Superstitions by a Peralta family is a contrivance of 20th century writers". A man named Miguel Peralta and his family did in fact operate a successful mine in the 1860s – but near Valanciana, California, not in Arizona. The mine was quite profitable, earning about $35,000 in less than one year; Blair describes this as "an unusually good return" for such a small gold mine to earn in such a relatively brief period. As of 1975, ruins of the Peralta mine were standing.

However, the Peralta Mine eventually became unprofitable and after the money was gone Miguel Peralta turned to fraud. Dr. George M. Willing Jr. paid Peralta $20,000 for the mining rights for an enormous swath of land – about 3,000,000 acres (12,000 km2) in southern Arizona and New Mexico – based on a deed originally granted by the Spanish Empire in the 18th century. Trouble came after Willing learned that the deed was entirely bogus. Despite his efforts, Willing was never able to recover the money he gave to Peralta. These deeds led to the basis of the James Reavis Arizona land swindle.

Blair argues that this Peralta story (well-known to Arizona residents) was eventually incorporated in the Lost Dutchman story, in a severely distorted version, following the renewed interest in the Lost Dutchman's mine in the 1930s.

The Truth about Dr. Thorne

Another detail which casts doubt on the story is the fact that, according to Blair, there was never any Dr. Thorne in the employ of the Army or indeed of the Federal Government in the 1860s. According to Blair, the origin of this story can be traced to a doctor named Thorne who was in private practice in New Mexico in the 1860s. Thorne claimed that he was taken captive by Navajos in 1854, and that during his captivity he had discovered a rich gold vein. Thorne related his claims to three U.S. soldiers in about 1858. The three soldiers set out to find the gold, but without success. Over the decades, this true tale was gradually absorbed into the Lost Dutchman's story.

The Lost Dutchman's Story

This tale involves two German men, Jacob Waltz (or Weitz, Weitzer, Walls, Welz, Walz, et cetera) and Jacob Weiser. However, Blair argues that there is a strong likelihood that there never was a second man named Weiser, but rather that a single person named Waltz (or a variant thereof) was, over the years, turned into two men as the legend of the Dutchman mine evolved. Blair contends that this story can be divided into "hawk" and "dove" versions, depending on if the German(s) are said to behave violently or peacefully. In most versions of the tale, Waltz and/or Weiser located a rich gold mine in the Superstition Mountains (in many versions of the story, they save or aid a member of the Peralta family, and are rewarded by being told the location of the mine). Weiser is attacked and wounded (whether by marauding Apaches or by a greedy Waltz), but survives at least long enough to tell a man called Dr. Walker about the mine. Waltz is also said to make a deathbed confession to Julia Thomas, and draws or describes a crude map to the gold mine.

Stories of the Soldiers' Lost Gold Vein

In yet another version of the tale, two (or more) U.S. Army soldiers are said to have discovered a vein of almost pure gold in or near the

Superstition Mountains. The soldiers are alleged to have presented some of the gold, but to have been killed or to have vanished soon after.

This account is usually dated to about 1870. According to Blair, the story may have its roots in the efforts of three U.S. soldiers to locate gold in an area of New Mexico, based on an allegedly true story related to them by Dr. Thorne of New Mexico.

The Historical Jacob Waltz

Blair cites ample evidence of the historical Jacob Waltz and suggests that there is additional evidence that supports the core elements of the story – that Waltz did in fact claim to have discovered (or at least heard the story of) a rich gold vein or cache. But Blair suggests that this core story was distorted in subsequent retellings, comparing the many variants of the Lost Dutchman's story to the game of Chinese whispers, where the original account is distorted in multiple retellings of the tale.

There was indeed a Jacob Waltz who immigrated to the U.S. from Germany. The earliest documentation of him in the U.S. is an 1848 affidavit in which Waltz declared himself to be "about 38 years old". A man called Jacob Walz was born in September 1810 in Württemberg. Blair suggests that this Waltz could be the same Waltz who later came to be regarded as the legendary Dutchman, and that he changed the spelling of his surname to better match its pronunciation.

Waltz relocated to Arizona in the 1860s, and stayed in the state for most of the rest of his life. He pursued mining and prospecting, but seems to have had little luck with either. In 1870, Waltz had a homestead of about 160 acres (0.65 km2) near Phoenix where he operated a farm.

There was a catastrophic flooding in Phoenix in 1891, and Waltz's farm was one of many that were devastated. Afterwards, Waltz fell ill (he was rumoured to have contracted pneumonia during the flooding). He died on October 25, 1891, after having been nursed by an acquaintance named Julia Thomas (she was usually described as a quadroon).

Blair suggests that there is little doubt that Waltz did in fact relate to Thomas the location of an alleged gold mine. As early as September 1, 1892, the Arizona Enterprise was reporting on the efforts of Thomas and several others to locate the lost mine whose location was told to her by Waltz. After this was unsuccessful, Thomas and her partners were reported to be selling maps to the mine for $7 each.

The Death of Adolph Ruth

Were it not for the death of amateur explorer and treasure hunter Adolph Ruth, the story of the Lost Dutchman's mine would have likely been little more than a footnote in Arizona history as one of hundreds of "lost mines" rumoured to be in the American West. Ruth disappeared while searching for the mine in the summer of 1931. His skull – with two bullet holes in it – was recovered about half a year after he vanished and the story made national news, thus sparking widespread interest in the Lost Dutchman's mine.

In a story that echoes some of the earlier tales, Ruth's son Erwin C. Ruth was said to have learned of the Peralta mine from a man called Pedro Gonzales (or Gonzalez). According to the story, in about 1912, Erwin C. Ruth gave some legal aid to Gonzales, saving him from almost certain imprisonment; in gratitude, Gonzales told Erwin about the Peralta mine in the Superstition Mountains, even reportedly passing on some antique maps of the site (Gonzales claimed to be descended from the Peralta family on his mother's side). Erwin passed the information to his father Adolph, who had a long-standing interest in lost mines and amateur exploration. In fact, the elder Ruth had fallen and badly broken several bones while seeking the lost Pegleg mine in California; he had metal pins in his leg, and used a cane to help him walk.

In June 1931, Ruth decided to finally try to locate the lost Peralta mine. After travelling to the region, Ruth stayed several days at the ranch of Tex Barkely and prepared for his expedition. Barkely repeatedly urged Ruth to abandon his search for the mine: the treacherous terrain of the Superstition Mountains could be difficult for experienced outdoorsmen, let alone for the 66-year-old Ruth.

However, Ruth ignored Barkely's advice, and set out for a two week stint in the mountains. Ruth did not return as scheduled, and no trace of him could be found after a brief search. In December, 1931, The Arizona Republic reported on the recent discovery of a human skull in the Superstition Mountains. To determine if the skull was Ruth's, it was examined by Dr. Ales Hrdlicka, a well-respected anthropologist who was also given several photos of Ruth, along with Ruth's dental records. As Curt Gentry writes, "Dr. Hrdlicka positively identified the skull as that of Adolph Ruth. He further stated, after examining the two holes in the skull, it appeared that a shotgun or high-powered rifle had been fired through the head at almost point-blank range, making the small hole when the bullet entered and the large hole when it exited."

In January 1932, human remains were discovered about three-quarters of a mile (1.21 km) from where the skull had been found. Though the remains had been scattered by scavengers, they were undoubtedly Ruth's: many of Ruth's personal effects were found at the scene, including a pistol (not missing any shells) and the metal pins used to mend his broken bones. But the map to the Peralta mine was said to be missing.

Tantalisingly, Ruth's checkbook was also recovered, and proved to contain a note written by Ruth wherein he claimed to have discovered the mine and gave detailed directions. Ruth ended his note with the phrase "Veni, vidi, vici".

Authorities in Arizona did not convene a criminal inquest regarding Ruth's death. They argued that Ruth had likely succumbed to thirst or heart disease though, as Gentry writes, "One official went so far as to suggest that Adolph Ruth might have committed suicide ... While this theory did not ignore the two holes in the skull, it did fail to explain how Ruth had managed to remove and bury the empty shell, then reload his gun, after shooting himself through the head." Blair notes that the conclusion of Arizona authorities was rejected by many, including Ruth's family, and also by "those who held onto the more romantic murdered-for-the-map story".

Blair writes that "the national wire services picked up the story (of Ruth's death) and ran it for more than it was worth", possibly seeing the mysterious story as a welcome reprieve from the bleak news that was otherwise typical of the Great Depression.

Other Deaths and Disappearances

Since Ruth's death, there have been several other allegedly mysterious deaths or encounters in the Superstition Mountains, but it's unclear how many of these can be regarded as reliably reported. Other searchers for the mine have disappeared in what have been reported as likely wilderness accidents.

- In the mid-1940s, the headless remains of prospector James A. Cravey were reportedly discovered in the Superstition Mountains. He'd allegedly disappeared after setting out to find the Lost Dutchman's mine.
- In his 1945 book about the Lost Dutchman's mine, Barry Storm claimed to have narrowly escaped from a mysterious sniper he dubbed "Mr. X". Storm further speculated that Adolph Ruth might have been a victim of the same sniper.
- In late November or early December 2009, Denver, Colorado resident Jesse Capen (35) went missing in the Tonto National Forest. His campsite was found abandoned, but he was not located. He was known to have been interested in the mine for years and had made previous trips to the area.
- On July 11, 2010, Utah hikers Curtis Merworth (49), Ardean Charles (66) and Malcolm Meeks (41) went missing in the Superstition Mountains looking for the mine. Merworth had become lost in the same area in 2009, requiring a rescue. On July 19, the Maricopa county Sheriff's department called off the search for the lost men. They presumably died in the summer heat. In January 2011, three sets of remains, believed to be those of the lost men, were recovered.

Treasure Maps, Codes and Ciphers

The Beale Cipher Treasure Mystery

The Beale ciphers are a set of three ciphertexts, one of which allegedly states the location of a buried treasure of gold and silver estimated to be worth over 30 million U.S. dollars in the present time. The other two ciphertexts allegedly describe the content of the treasure, and list the names of the treasure-owners' next of kin, respectively. The story of the three ciphertexts originates from an 1885 pamphlet detailing treasure being buried by a man named Thomas Jefferson Beale in a secret location in Virginia in 1820. Beale entrusted the box containing the encrypted messages with a local innkeeper named Robert Morriss and then disappeared, never to be seen again. The innkeeper gave the three encrypted ciphertexts to a friend before he died. The friend then spent the next twenty years of his life trying to decode the messages, and was able to solve only one of them which gave details of the treasure buried and the general location of the treasure. Since the publication of the pamphlet, a number of attempts have been made to decode the two remaining ciphertexts and to find the treasure, but all have resulted in failure.

The Story

It is important to note that all of the following information originates from one source – a single pamphlet published in 1885, entitled 'The Beale Papers'.

The treasure was said to have been obtained by an American man named Thomas Jefferson Beale in 1818 (one of Beale's letters suggests crevice mining of metallic gold, somewhat implausibly in the claimed terrain, but nothing else is known) somewhere in what is now the American Southwest. Where exactly the treasure was found is unknown, but speculation centres to the north of Santa Fe, New

Beale Vault

Mexico, based on one of Beale's letters. Beale led about 30 adventures on the discovery, but no solid proof of either Beale, or any of his men's existence has yet been found in any public or private record.

It is claimed that Beale placed the ciphertexts in an iron box, and left it with a reliable person in 1822, a Lynchburg innkeeper, Robert Morriss, near Montvale in Bedford County, Virginia (where the treasure is said to have been buried). Beale asked him not to open that box, unless he didn't return from his journey before 10 years. Beale promised to mail Morriss the keys, but they were never received; perhaps Beale died before he could do so. Morriss, in 1832, opened the box and unsuccessfully attempted to solve the ciphers on his own but, decades later, passed the box and contents (three letters and three ciphertexts), and the story, to one of his friends.

Using a particular edition of the United States Declaration of Independence as the key for a book cipher, the friend successfully deciphered the second ciphertext, which gave descriptions of the buried treasure. The friend ultimately made the letters and ciphertexts public, apparently via James B Ward, in an 1885 pamphlet entitled 'The Beale Papers'. Ward is thus apparently not 'the friend'. Ward himself is obscure, and is untraceable in local records with the exception that someone of that name was the owner of the home in which a Sarah Morriss, identified as the consort of Robert Morriss, died at 77 (Lynchburg Virginian newspaper, May 21, 1861), so perhaps he was 'the friend' after all. There was no explanation of the accident which led to the solution of the second ciphertext, which perhaps suggests that there was additional information now lost (from Morriss).

The Deciphered Message

The plaintext reads:

I have deposited in the county of Bedford, about four miles from Buford's, in an excavation or vault, six feet below the surface of the ground, the following articles, belonging jointly to the parties whose names are given in number '3,' herewith:

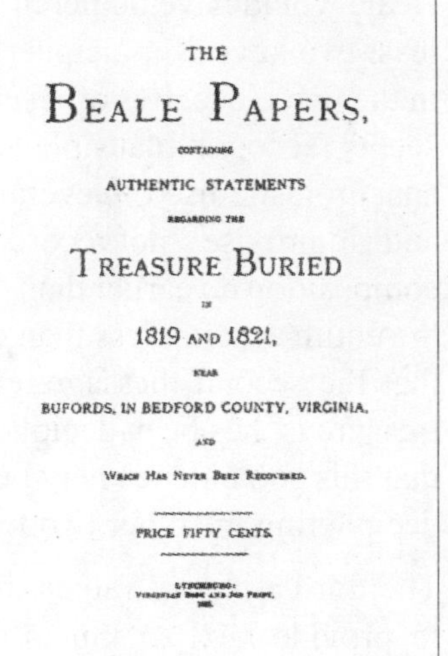
THE

BEALE PAPERS,

CONTAINING

AUTHENTIC STATEMENTS

REGARDING THE

TREASURE BURIED

IN

1819 AND 1821,

NEAR

BUFORDS, IN BEDFORD COUNTY, VIRGINIA,

AND

WHICH HAS NEVER BEEN RECOVERED.

PRICE FIFTY CENTS.

The Beale Papers

The first deposit consisted of ten hundred and fourteen pounds of gold, and thirty-eight hundred and twelve pounds of silver, deposited Nov. eighteen nineteen. The second was made December, 1821, and consisted of nineteen hundred and seven pounds of gold, and twelve hundred and eighty-eight pounds of silver; also jewels, obtained in St. Louis in exchange for silver to save transportation, and valued at US$13,000.

The above is securely packed in iron pots, with iron covers. The vault is roughly lined with stone, and the vessels rest on solid stone, and are covered with others. Paper number '1' describes the exact locality of the vault, so that no difficulty will be had in finding it.

The second cipher can be decrypted fairly easily using any copy of the United States Declaration of Independence, but some editing for spelling is necessary.

Truth or Hoax?

There has been considerable debate over whether the remaining two ciphertexts are real or hoaxes.

In 1934, Dr. Clarence Williams, a researcher at the Library of Congress, said, 'To me, the pamphlet story has all the earmarks of a fake . . . There was no evidence to save the word of the unknown author of the pamphlet that he ever had the papers.'

The pamphlet's background story has several implausibility's, and is based almost entirely on circumstantial evidence and hearsay. Many cryptographers have also claimed that the two remaining ciphertexts have statistical characteristics which suggest that they are not actually encryptions of an English plain text. Others have also questioned why

Beale would have bothered writing three different ciphertexts (with at least two keys, if not ciphers) for what is essentially a single message in the first place. It is often claimed that, in many ways, the entire story seems far too implausible to be true. Some observers have noted that anachronistic use of several English terms (e.g. the word 'stampede' and 'improvise', not recorded before the 1840s) in the letters suggest composition no earlier than the 1840s, not the early 1820s, thus making the entire account less than credible. It is also interesting, some claim, that the second message, containing the information as to what the treasure is, has been deciphered, but the others have not. They believe that this coincidence may be a deliberate ploy to encourage interest in deciphering the other two texts, only to discover they are hoaxes.

The third cipher is rather short, especially considering it is supposed to provide next of kin information for 30 individuals. Some have suggested that the ciphers may be legitimate codes, but do not actually contain any relevant information once 'cracked' and instead simply reveal a prank message of some sort.

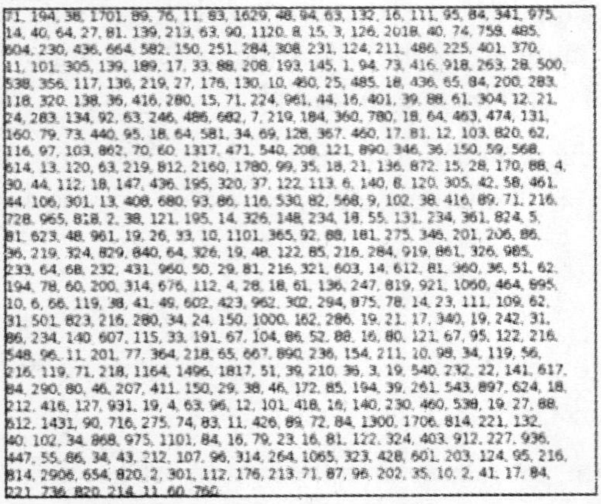

71, 194, 38, 1701, 89, 76, 11, 83, 1629, 48, 94, 63, 132, 16, 111, 95, 84, 341, 975,
14, 40, 64, 27, 81, 139, 213, 63, 90, 1120, 8, 15, 3, 126, 2018, 40, 74, 758, 485,
604, 230, 436, 664, 582, 150, 251, 284, 308, 231, 124, 211, 486, 225, 401, 370,
11, 101, 305, 139, 189, 17, 33, 88, 208, 193, 145, 1, 94, 73, 416, 918, 263, 28, 500,
538, 356, 117, 136, 219, 27, 176, 130, 10, 460, 25, 485, 18, 436, 65, 84, 200, 283,
118, 320, 138, 36, 416, 280, 15, 71, 224, 961, 44, 16, 401, 39, 88, 61, 304, 12, 21,
24, 283, 134, 92, 63, 246, 486, 682, 7, 219, 184, 360, 780, 18, 64, 463, 474, 131,
160, 79, 73, 440, 95, 18, 64, 581, 34, 69, 128, 367, 460, 17, 81, 12, 103, 820, 62,
116, 97, 103, 862, 70, 60, 1317, 471, 540, 208, 121, 890, 346, 36, 150, 59, 568,
614, 13, 120, 63, 219, 812, 2160, 1780, 99, 35, 18, 21, 136, 872, 15, 28, 170, 88, 4,
30, 44, 112, 18, 147, 436, 195, 320, 37, 122, 113, 6, 140, 8, 120, 305, 42, 58, 461,
44, 106, 301, 13, 408, 680, 93, 86, 116, 530, 82, 568, 9, 102, 38, 416, 89, 71, 216,
728, 965, 818, 2, 38, 121, 195, 14, 326, 148, 234, 18, 55, 131, 234, 361, 824, 5,
81, 623, 48, 961, 19, 26, 33, 10, 1101, 365, 92, 88, 181, 275, 346, 201, 206, 86,
36, 219, 324, 829, 840, 64, 326, 19, 48, 122, 85, 216, 284, 919, 861, 326, 985,
233, 64, 68, 232, 431, 960, 50, 29, 81, 216, 321, 603, 14, 612, 81, 360, 36, 51, 62,
194, 78, 60, 200, 314, 676, 112, 4, 28, 18, 61, 136, 247, 819, 921, 1060, 464, 895,
10, 6, 66, 119, 38, 41, 49, 602, 423, 962, 302, 294, 875, 78, 14, 23, 111, 109, 62,
31, 501, 823, 216, 280, 34, 24, 150, 1000, 162, 286, 19, 21, 17, 340, 19, 242, 31,
86, 234, 140, 607, 115, 33, 191, 67, 104, 86, 52, 88, 16, 80, 121, 67, 95, 122, 216,
548, 96, 11, 201, 77, 364, 218, 65, 667, 890, 236, 154, 211, 10, 98, 34, 119, 56,
216, 119, 71, 218, 1164, 1496, 1817, 51, 39, 210, 36, 3, 19, 540, 232, 22, 141, 617,
84, 290, 80, 46, 207, 411, 150, 29, 38, 46, 172, 85, 194, 39, 261, 543, 897, 624, 18,
212, 416, 127, 931, 19, 4, 63, 96, 12, 101, 418, 16, 140, 230, 460, 538, 19, 27, 88,
612, 1431, 90, 716, 275, 74, 83, 11, 426, 89, 72, 84, 1300, 1706, 814, 221, 132,
40, 102, 34, 868, 975, 1101, 84, 16, 79, 23, 16, 81, 122, 324, 403, 912, 227, 936,
447, 55, 86, 34, 43, 212, 107, 96, 314, 264, 1065, 323, 428, 601, 203, 124, 95, 216,
814, 2906, 654, 820, 2, 301, 112, 176, 213, 71, 87, 96, 202, 35, 10, 2, 41, 17, 84,
221, 736, 820, 214, 11, 60, 760.

Beale Cipher

Regardless, there have been many attempts to break the remaining cipher(s). Most attempts have tried other historical texts as keys (eg, the Magna Carta, various books of the Bible, the U.S. Constitution, the Virginia Royal Charter, etc), assuming the ciphertexts were produced with some book cipher, but none have been recognised as successful to date. Breaking the cipher(s) may depend on random chance (as, for instance, stumbling upon a book key if the two remaining cyphertexts are actually book ciphers); so far, even the most skilled cryptanalysts who have attempted them have been defeated.

Did Thomas J. Beale Exist?

A survey of U.S. Census records in 1810 shows two persons named Thomas Beale, in Connecticut and New Hampshire. However, the population schedules from the 1810 U.S. Census are completely missing for seven states, one territory, the District of Columbia, and 18 of the counties of Virginia. The 1820 U.S. Census has two persons named Thomas Beale, in Louisiana and Tennessee, and a Thomas K. Beale in Virginia. But the population schedules are completely missing for three states and one territory.

Before 1850, the U.S. Census recorded the names of only the heads of households; others in the household were only counted, and if he existed, Beale may have been living in someone else's household.

Digging for Treasure in Bedford County

Doubts have not deterred many treasure hunters, however. The 'information' that there is buried treasure in Bedford County has stimulated many an expedition with shovels, and other implements of discovery, looking for likely spots. For more than a hundred years, people have been arrested for trespassing and unauthorised digging; some of them in groups as in the case of some folks from Pennsylvania in the 1990s. The number of man-made holes (up to 'six feet deep' or so) in Bedford County is said to be extraordinarily large; some get filled in, some don't. County inhabitants are said to now lack enthusiasm and to generally view people with metal detectors with disfavour.

There is reportedly a story of a woman digging up a cemetery because she was convinced that Beale had hid the treasure there.

The story has been the subject of at least two television documentaries (one is in the UK's Mystery series), several books, and considerable Internet activity. There is even a 2001 claim (and supporting Website) of having decrypted one of the remaining cipher texts and of finding the Beale vault – minus its supposed treasure (and any explanation of the cryptanalysis).

Yamashita's Gold – The Treasure of 'The Tiger of Malaya'

Yamashita's gold, also referred to as the Yamashita treasure, is the name given to the alleged war loot stolen in Southeast Asia by Japanese forces during World War II and hidden in caves, tunnels and underground complexes in the Philippines. It is named for the Japanese General Tomoyuki Yamashita, nicknamed "The Tiger of Malaya". Though accounts that the treasure remains hidden in Philippines have lured treasure-hunters from around the world for over fifty years, its existence is discounted by most experts. The rumoured treasure has been the subject of a complex lawsuit that was filed in a Hawaiian state court in 1988 involving a Filipino treasure hunter, Rogelio Roxas, and the former Philippine president, Ferdinand Marcos.

Looting and Alleged Cover-up

Yamashita

ChichibunomiyaYamashita

Prominent among those arguing for the existence of Yamashita's gold are Sterling Seagrave and Peggy Seagrave, who have written two books relating to the subject – *The Yamato Dynasty: the Secret History of Japan's Imperial Family* (2000) and *Gold Warriors: America's Secret Recovery of Yamashita's Gold* (2003). The Seagraves contend that looting was organised on a massive scale, by both yakuza gangsters such as Yoshio Kodama, and the highest levels of Japanese society, including Emperor Hirohito. The Japanese government intended that loot from Southeast Asia would finance Japan's war effort. The Seagraves allege that Hirohito appointed his brother, Prince Yasuhito Chichibu, to head a secret organisation called Kin no yuri ("Golden Lily"), for this purpose. It is purported that many of those who knew the locations of the loot were killed during the war, or later tried by the Allies for war crimes and executed or incarcerated. Yamashita himself was executed by the U.S. Army for his war crimes on February 23, 1946.

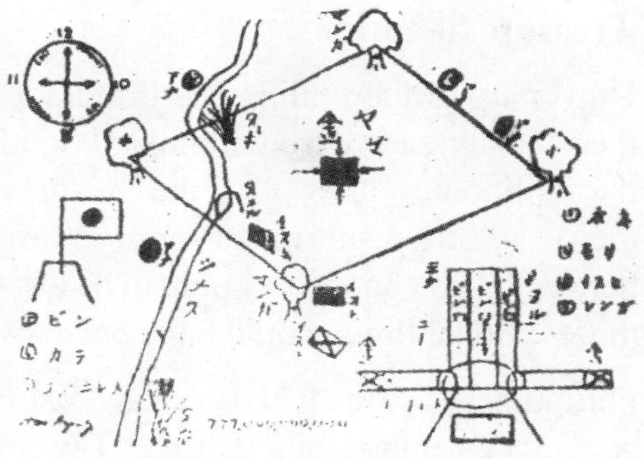

Yamashita Treasure Map

The stolen property reportedly included many different kinds of valuables looted from banks, depositories, temples, churches, other commercial premises, mosques, museums and private homes. It takes its name from General Tomoyuki Yamashita, who assumed command of Japanese forces in the Philippines in 1944.

According to various accounts, the loot was initially concentrated in Singapore, and later transported to the Philippines. The Japanese hoped to ship the treasure from the Philippines to the Japanese Home Islands after the war ended. As the War in the Pacific progressed, U.S. Navy submarines and Allied warplanes inflicted increasingly heavy sinkings of Japanese merchant shipping. Some of the ships carrying the war booty back to Japan were sunk in combat.

The Seagraves and a few others have claimed that American military intelligence operatives located much of the loot; they colluded with Hirohito and other senior Japanese figures to conceal its existence, and; they used it to finance American covert intelligence operations around the world during the Cold War. These rumours have inspired many hopeful treasure hunters, but most experts and Filipino historians say there is no credible evidence behind these claims.

In 1992, Imelda Marcos claimed that Yamashita's gold accounted for the bulk of the wealth of her husband, Ferdinand Marcos.

Many individuals and consortia, both Philippine and foreign, continue to search for treasure sites. A number of accidental deaths, injuries and financial losses incurred by treasure hunters have been reported.

At present, the Mines and Geosciences Bureau of the Department of Natural Resources of the Philippines is the Filipino government agency that grants treasure permits.

Treasure Skeptics

University of the Philippines Professor Rico Jose has questioned the theory that treasure from mainland South East Asia was transported to the Philippines: "By 1943, the Japanese were no longer in control of the seas... It doesn't make sense to bring in something that valuable here when you know it's going to be lost to the Americans anyway. The more rational thing would have been to send it to Taiwan or China."

Philippines National Historical Institute chairman and historian Ambeth Ocampo commented: "Two of the wealth myths I usually encounter are the Yamashita treasure and gossip that the Cojuangco fortune was founded on a bag of money…" Ocampo also said: "For the past 50 years many people, both Filipinos and foreigners, have spent their time, money and energy in search of Yamashita's elusive treasure." Professor Ocampo noted, "What makes me wonder is that for the past 50 years, despite all the treasure hunters, their maps, oral testimony and sophisticated metal detectors, nobody has found a thing."

Rogelio Roxas Lawsuit

In March 1988, a Filipino treasure hunter named Rogelio Roxas filed a lawsuit in the state of Hawaii against the former President of the Philippines, Ferdinand Marcos and his wife Imelda Marcos for theft and human rights abuses. Roxas claimed that in Baguio City in 1961, he met the son of a former member of the Japanese army who mapped for him the location of the legendary Yamashita Treasure. Roxas claimed a second man, who served as Yamashita's interpreter during the Second World War, told him of visiting an underground chamber there where stores of gold and silver were kept, and who told of a golden buddha kept at a convent located near the underground chambers. Roxas claimed that within the next few years he formed a group to search for the treasure, and obtained a permit for the purpose from a relative of Ferdinand, Judge Pio Marcos. In 1971, Roxas claimed, he and his group uncovered an enclosed chamber on state lands near Baguio City where he found bayonets, samurai swords, radios, and skeletal remains dressed in a Japanese military uniform. Also found in the chamber, Roxas claimed, were a 3-foot-high (0.91 m) golden-coloured Buddha and numerous stacked crates which filled an area approximately 6 feet x 6 feet x 35 feet. He claimed he opened just one of the boxes, and found it packed with gold bullion. He said he took from the chamber the golden Buddha, which he estimated to weigh 1,000 kilograms, and one box with twenty-four gold bars, and hid them in his home. He claimed he resealed the chamber for safekeeping until he could arrange the removal of the remaining boxes, which he suspected were also filled with gold bars. Roxas said he sold seven of the gold bars from the opened box, and sought potential buyers for the golden Buddha. Two individuals representing prospective buyers examined and tested the metal in the Buddha, Roxas said, and reported it was made of solid, 20-carat gold. It was soon after this, Roxas claimed, that President Ferdinand Marcos learned of Roxas' discovery and ordered him arrested, beaten, and the Buddha and remaining gold seized. Roxas alleged that in retaliation to his vocal campaign to reclaim the Buddha and the remainder of the treasure taken from him, Ferdinand continued to have Roxas threatened, beaten and eventually incarcerated for over a year.

Following his release, Roxas put his claims against Marcos on hold until Ferdinand lost the presidency in 1986. But in 1988, Roxas and the Golden Budha Corporation, which now held the ownership rights to the treasure Roxas claims was stolen from him, filed suit against Ferdinand and wife Imelda in a Hawaiian state court seeking damages for the theft and the surrounding human rights abuses committed against Roxas. Roxas died on the eve of trial, but prior to his death he gave the deposition testimony that would be later used in evidence. In 1996, the Roxas estate and the Golden Budha Corporation received what was then largest judgment ever awarded in history, $22 billion which with interest increased to $40.5 billion. In 1998, The Hawaii Supreme Court held that there was sufficient evidence to support the jury's finding that Roxas found the treasure and that Marcos converted it. However, the court reversed the damage award, holding that the $22 billion award of damages for the chamber full of gold was too speculative, as there was no evidence of quantity or quality, and ordered a new hearing on the value of the golden Buddha and 17 bars of gold only. After several more years of legal proceedings, the Golden Budha Corporation obtained a final judgment against Imelda Marcos to the extent of her interest in the Marcos estate in the principal amount of $13,275,848.37 and Roxas' estate obtained a $6 million judgment on the claim for human right abuse.

This lawsuit ultimately concluded that Roxas found a treasure, and although the Hawaiian state court was not required to determine whether this particular treasure was the legendary Yamashita's gold, the testimony relied upon by the court in reaching its conclusion pointed in that direction. Roxas was allegedly following a map from the son of a Japanese soldier; Roxas allegedly relied on tips provided from Yamashita's interpreter; and Roxas allegedly found samurai swords and the skeletons of dead Japanese soldiers in the treasure chamber. All this led the United States Ninth Circuit Court of Appeal to summarise the allegations leading to Roxas' final judgment as follows: "The Yamashita Treasure was found by Roxas and stolen from Roxas by Marcos' men."

Nazi Gold – The Missing Spoils of War

1 Hidden Nazi Gold in the Mountains Of Austria

As World War II drew to a close, Hitler is said to have ordered his elite soldiers, the notorious elite Schutzstaffel (the SS), to make a last stand in the mountains of Austria, the impenetrable Alps being the perfect base from which to fight a prolonged guerrilla war.

Networks of tunnels had already been prepared. They had originally been piled high with all the war materials and supplies the SS would need, it was even rumoured that large underground arms and munitions factories had been constructed.

However, supply difficulties and the continued Allied bombing of Germany's industrial centres meant that by the time the end came, all the supplies in the National Redoubt were long gone and the SS had been smashed by the approaching Allied and Soviet forces. They would never get to make their last stand in the Alpenfestung (Alpine Fortress).

Hitler's armies had spent years looting the treasuries and museums of the countries they had conquered, wealthy Jews had their possessions, property and art collections confiscated.

The Nazi high command, realising that defeat was inevitable, decided to ensure that the looted treasures would not fall into the hands of the rapidly advancing allies or soviets and hid the gold and art treasures in the tunnels of the National Redoubt.

Nazi Gold – Austria

As the saying goes, 'Don't put all of your eggs in one basket,' the treasures were split up and hidden in many tunnel systems in the mountains, and although some of these treasure and art caches were discovered by advancing allied troops (such as the Merkers mine treasure), others weren't and remain undiscovered in the Alps to this day.

Reality

The Allied high command certainly believed the National Redoubt existed and it seems many Nazis did too, but ultimately it was a myth. The Nazis had been planning an evacuation of high ranking political and military figures to the Redoubt, but the operation was not approved by Hitler.

The National Redoubt plan was seized upon by the minister for propaganda, Joseph Goebbels, and tales of its existence became completely blown out of all proportion.

The last stand did happen, but not in the mountains of southern Germany and Austria and it was nowhere near as effective as Hitler and his Generals would have liked, nor was any kind of continuation government established in the Redoubt.

A great deal of the material looted by the Nazis is still missing, that is a fact, the big question is what happened to it. Was it destroyed in allied bombing raids? Is it still hidden in a mine or tunnel somewhere? Many claim that the bulk of the missing art and gold is in Russia, removed by the Red Army under the orders of Joseph Stalin. None or all of these answers may be true.

Nazi Gold Recovered

The largest single cache of gold and art was not found in a secret underground fortress, but in a salt mine near the village of Merkers. It seems that the Merkers salt mine was first used as a store for gold and art in March 1945 when the Germans sought a safe place for the art and wealth of the Reichsbank, away from the non-stop bombing and shelling. Other locations had been considered, but were found to be too damp for storing important paintings and the huge quantities of banknotes.

Nazi Gold Recovery

The Merkers treasure was captured by the Americans on the 7th of April 1945. Generals Dwight D. Eisenhower, George S. Patton and Omar N. Bradley visited the mine soon after its discovery to inspect the treasure and to ensure its safe removal to another secure location away from the rapidly advancing Soviets, the allies feared the loss of the art and gold to the Russians as much as the Germans did.

The Merkers Mine

Partial list of material recovered from the Merkers mine is as follows:

• 8,198 bars of gold bullion • 55 boxes of crated gold bullion • 1,300 bags of gold Reichsmarks • 711 bags of American twenty-dollar gold pieces • billion Reichsmarks • 20 silver bars • 40 bags containing silver bars • 63 boxes and 55 bags of silver plate • 1 bag containing six platinum bars

The SS Deaths Head Treasure

The mountains around Wewelsburg castle in North Rhine-Westphalia (Nordrhein-Westfalen) may still be home to a treasure of great value that was concealed there by the SS at the end of World War II.

The SS Ehrenring (SS Honour Ring) or Totenkopfrinzg (Death's Head Ring) was given to members of the SS as an award for bravery. Upon the death of the recipient, the rings were to be returned to Wewelsburg castle, the 'spiritual home' of the SS. The rings were made of silver and manufactured by Gahr & Co. of Munich.

Death's Head Rings

As the war drew to a close, Himmler ordered that all of the rings that had been returned (around 9,280) to castle should be hidden in a cave somewhere near Wewelsburg and the entrance to the cave sealed forever with explosives.

Assuming that former SS members did not return and recovered the rings after the war, the rings could still be hidden on a mountain somewhere near Wewelsburg castle today.

At current market values, the rings would be worth between £3,000 and £5,000 each, or £27,840,000 - £46,400,000 in total.

Although, if the hoard were ever to make it to the open market, they would no longer be rare, and their value would be dramatically reduced.

The rings held at the castle were only those that were returned there from the battlefields, in many cases soldiers' remains were not recovered, or rings were lost, so genuine examples of Totenkopfring's do turn up occasionally.

Lake Toplitz Treasure

Lake Toplitz is a lake situated in a dense mountain forest high up in the Austrian Alps, 60 miles from Salzburg city in western Austria. It is surrounded by cliffs and forests in the picturesque Salzkammergut lake district within the Totes Gebirge, or dead mountains.

It is believed that the lake carries the past misdeeds of Germany in World War II. Supposedly, the Nazis stashed vast quantities of gold and other priceless plunder, including the lost panels from Russia's Amber Room, as well as documents detailing the whereabouts of other Third Reich caches.

It has also been reported that after the war, former SS member employed divers to try, locate and salvage a number of sealed tubes from the depths of the lake, the tubes were said to contain details of secret Nazi bank accounts in Switzerland.

Millions of counterfeit pound sterling notes were also dumped in the lake as a cover up act after a strategy called Operation Bernhard was never put into action. American documentary makers using a mini submarine actually managed to recover some of the banknotes from the lake bottom.

During the war, in the years 1943 and 1944, the shore of Lake Toplitz served as home to a Nazi naval testing station, only accessible on foot by a hazardous mile-long path. Using copper diaphragms, scientists experimented with different explosives, detonating up to 4,000 kg charges at various depths. They also fired torpedoes from a launching pad in the lake into the Tote Mountains, producing vast holes in the canyon walls. This testing has left behind another hazard for any treasure hunter exploring the depths – countless tons of unexploded ordinance.

The Gold of the Oradour-sur-Glane Massacre

As an Allied attack on Europe loomed, the local French Resistance increased its activities in order to occupy the German forces and hinder communications.

2nd SS Panzer Division 'Das Reich' was ordered to make its way across country to the fighting in Normandy. Along the way, it came under constant attack and sabotage from the French Resistance. Allegedly, SS soldiers were further angered by finding atrocities committed by some resistance; in particular, a German ambulance in which all the wounded had been killed and the driver and assistants tied to the cab before the vehicle was set on fire. No record of this alleged incident exists in German records.

Early on the morning of June 10, Sturmbannführer Adolf Diekmann reported to Sturmbannführer Otto Weidinger that he had been approached by two French civilians who claimed that a high German official was being held by the French Resistance guerrilla, the Maquis, in Oradour. That day, he was to be executed and publicly burnt amidst celebrations. The two French civilians also stated that the whole population was working with the Maquis and that high ranking leaders were there at the moment. At about the same time, the SD in Limoges reported that their local informers had reported a Maquis headquarters in Oradour. The high German official was believed to be Sturmbannfuhrer Helmut Kampfe, a personal friend of both Diekmann and Weidinger who had been captured by the Maquis the day before. Kampfe was never found and is listed in SS records as 'Missing in southern France in action against terrorists'.

On June 10, the 1st battalion of the Waffen-SS (Der Führer) regiment, led by Sturmbannführer Otto Dickmann, encircled the town of Oradour-sur-Glane and ordered all the inhabitants to congregate in a public fairground near the village centre, ostensibly to examine people's papers. All the women and children were taken to the church, while the village was looted. Meanwhile, the men were taken to six barns where machine gun nests were already in place. According to the account of a survivor, the soldiers began shooting at them, aiming for their legs so that they would die more slowly. Once the victims were no longer able to move, the soldiers covered their bodies with kindling and set the barns on fire. Only five men escaped; 197 died there.

Town of Oradour-sur-Glane

Having finished with the men, the soldiers then entered the church and put an incendiary device in place. After it was ignited, the surviving women and children tried to flee from the doors and windows but were met with machine gun fire. Only one woman survived; another 240 women and 205 children died in the mayhem. Another small group of about twenty villagers had fled Oradour as soon as the soldiers appeared. That night the remainder of the village was razed. A few days later the survivors were allowed to bury the dead.

Oradour-sur-Glane Massacre

Post-war Outcomes

On January 12, 1953, a trial began against the surviving 65 of the about 200 soldiers before a military tribunal in Bordeaux. Only 21 of them were present (many living in Germany would not be extradited). Among them were 7 Germans, the 14 others were Alsatians, i.e. French nationals who were members of the SS Division 'Reich'. All but one of them claimed to have been drafted into the Waffen-SS against their will (the so-called malgré-nous). The SS records do not show that any such drafting took place. It is most likely that the Alsatians were Nazi sympathisers and volunteered.

This caused huge protest in Alsace, forcing the French authorities to split the process in two separate ones according to the nationality of the defendants. On February 11, 20 defendants were found guilty. Continuing uproar (including calls for autonomy) in Alsace pressed the French parliament to pass an amnesty law for all malgré-nous on February 19, and the convicted Alsatians were released shortly afterwards. This in turn caused bitter protest in the Limousin region.

By 1958, all the German defendants had been released as well. General Karl-Heinz Lammerding of the Das Reich division, who had given the orders for the measures against the Resistance, died in 1971 after a successful entrepreneurial career, never having been indicted.

The last trial against a former Waffen-SS member took place in 1983. Shortly before, in the GDR the former SS-Obersturmführer Heinz Barth had been tracked down. Barth participated in the Oradour massacre as a platoon leader in the regiment 'Der Führer', commanding 45 soldiers. He was amongst other war crimes charged with having given orders to shoot 20 men in a garage. Barth was sentenced to life imprisonment by the 1st senate of the city court Berlin. He was released from prison in the re-unified Germany in 1997.

After the war, General Charles de Gaulle decided that the village would never be rebuilt. Instead, it would remain as a memorial to the cruelty of Nazi occupation. In 1999, President Jacques Chirac dedicated a visitors' centre, the centre de la mémoire, in Oradour-sur-Glane and named the site a Village Martyr.

The Oradour-sur-Glane Massacre was one of the great horrors of World War II. 642 unarmed men, women and children were slaughtered by the Der Führer regiment of 2nd SS Panzer Division, Das Reich led by Sturmbannführer Adolf Diekmann.

The Alleged Gold of Oradour

In 1988, a new spin was put on the story of the Oradour-sur-Glane massacre when a British man named Robin Mackness released a book telling the story of how he went from working in a comfortable job for a Swiss bank to an unpleasant prison cell in France.

In 1982, Mackness was asked by a colleague at the bank, Jamie Baruch, to meet a man named Raoul Denis who had a large quantity of gold that he wanted to move to Switzerland.

Raoul Denis claimed to be one of the few survivors of the Oradour-sur-Glane massacre, but he told a story very different to the widely excepted history. According to Raoul, the massacre was not a reprisal for the death of a high ranking German officer but was an attempt by Das Reich to recover a shipment of gold which had been stolen from a convoy that had been attacked by members of the French Resistance.

Raoul claimed that he was a member of the resistance cell that had ambushed the German convoy and that he and a German soldier were the only survivors of the ensuing fire fight, the soldier escaped leaving Raoul with what was left of the convoy.

Raoul found one of the trucks in the convoy piled high with filing cabinets and heavy boxes which contained gold bars. Realising that he was alone with no transport, he buried the gold in the corner of a nearby field and set what was left of the convoy ablaze.

The Germans were quick to notice the loss of the gold shipment and sent troops to the area of the ambush and to the nearest village – Oradour-sur-Glane.

The troops rounded up the villagers, examined their identity papers and then began interrogations to try and learn the location of the gold, but Raoul was the only person who knew where it was and he was not in the village at that time. The German troops, unable to get the locals to tell them where the gold was, massacred the town's population.

Raoul claimed that he recovered the gold from the field at the end of the war, used some of it, set a business and hid the rest.

Raoul wanted Mackness to smuggle the the gold from France to Switzerland, after hearing his story Mackness agreed and loaded 20 bars of gold into his car. On route to Switzerland, Mackness was pulled over by French Customs officials and his car was searched. He managed to escape only to be caught by armed officers in a nearby village, a photograph in his book shows a number of bullet holes in the BMW 735i Mackness claims to have been driving at the time of his capture.

Mackness refused to name Raoul in court and was sentenced to 18 months imprisonment and fined 8 million Francs (reduced to 80,000f on appeal). His employers, 'BanqueLéman', refused to cooperate with the French authorities and basically left him rot. The bank did, however, refund Raoul the full value of the gold the French had seized.

Mackness claims that Raoul died of cancer before his release from prison in 1984. After he was released, Mackness contacted Raoul's family who denied any knowledge of what had happened to him and denied all knowledge of the gold.

Why did Raoul claim that the gold had originated from the Oradour-sur-Glane Massacre?

The most obvious answer to this is that the gold did genuinely have a Nazi/SS pedigree and he needed to explain how he got it without admitting its actual history.

Gold bars have markings and serial numbers, markings and serial numbers can be traced, what if the current holders of the gold tried to sell it but the markings and serial numbers proved that the original owners were the Reichsbank, circa 1944, or even worse, that the bars could be traced directly back to the SS.

It might seem to many, a small justice that the descendants of the very few survivors of the massacre still had the gold – they had paid for it in blood so why shouldn't they be allowed to keep it?

What is the 'Oradour Gold's' True History?

According to Mackness, he didn't doubt its Nazi vintage given that much of it bore Reichsbank stamps, the gold could have been from one of the many caches of gold that where hidden as the 'thousand year Reich' crumbled. It may have been recovered soon after the war ended or even many years later.

Although he was not a betting man, he would lay money on the gold having been stored in Spain. After the war so many high ranking Nazi's settled there, including the infamous 'Commando Extraordinaire' Otto Skorzeny.

These men were used to living the high life, not only would they have needed money to establish themselves in a new country (a house, a business etc.) but they would certainly have also wanted the finer things in life that they had become accustomed to as Hitler's trusted henchmen, and by all accounts they got them.

Spain was also believed by many intelligence officers to be a major centre for the ODESSA network, indeed, Otto Skorzeny was believed to have been the head of ODESSA right up until his death in Spain in 1975.

Another possibility was that the gold had been in the keeping of a stay behind in France since World War II.

Problems:

1) Robin Mackness used pseudonyms for all the players in story making fact checking very difficult or even impossible, even the name of the bank he worked for, Banque Léman, was a pseudonym.
2) 'Raoul Denis' was the only person to have told the gold-theft version of the story of the Oradour-sur-Glane massacre.
3) There seemed to be no evidence that a German convoy was ambushed anywhere near Oradour around the time period claimed by Raoul – gold carrying or not.

The Amber Room – Russia's Greatest Lost Treasure

The Amber Room (German Bernsteinzimmer) in the Catherine Palace of Tsarskoe Selo near Saint Petersburg is a complete chamber decoration of amber panels backed with gold leaf and mirrors. Due to its singular beauty, it was sometimes dubbed the 'Eighth Wonder of the World'.

It was created in the beginning of 18th century in Prussia. Soon after its creation, it was given by the Prussian king, Friedrich Wilhelm I, to his then ally, Tsar Peter the Great of the Russian Empire.

The Amber Room was looted during World War II by Nazi Germany, and knowledge of its whereabouts was lost in the chaos at the end of the war. Its exact fate remains a mystery to this day, and the search for it has been one of the greatest treasure hunts of all time.

It was made in 1701 in order to be installed at Charlottenburg Palace, home of Friedrich I, the first king of Prussia, at the urging of his second wife, Sophie Charlotte. The concept of the room and its design was by Andreas Schlüter. It was crafted by Gottfried Wolfram, master craftsman to the Danish court of King Frederick IV of Denmark, with help from the amber masters Ernst Schacht and Gottfried Turau from Danzig (Gdańsk).

It did not, however, remain at Charlottenburg for long. Peter the Great admired it on a visit and in 1716, Friedrich Wilhelm I, the first king's son, presented it to him, and with that act cemented a Prussian-Russian alliance against Sweden.

The Amber Room (a rare picture)

In 1755, Tsarina Elizabeth Petrovna had it transferred and installed, first in the Winter Palace, and then in the Catherine Palace. From Berlin,

Frederick II the Great sent her more Baltic amber, in order to fill out the originals in the new design by the tsarina's Italian court architect, Bartolomeo Rastrelli.

The Amber Room represented a joint effort of German and Russian craftsmen. After several other 18th-century renovations, it covered more than 55 square metres and contained over six tonnes of amber. It took over ten years to construct.

Looted by Nazis

Shortly after the beginning of German invasion of the Soviet Union in World War II (Operation Barbarossa), the curators responsible for removing the art treasures of Leningrad tried to disassemble the Amber Room, so it could be removed to safety. However, over the years the amber had dried out and become brittle, so that when they tried to remove it, the fragile amber started to crumble. The Amber Room was therefore hidden behind mundane wallpaper, in an attempt to keep Nazi forces from seizing it.

However, these attempts failed: the Nazis disassembled the Amber Room, and removed it to Königsberg, (renamed Kaliningrad in 1946), in East Prussia, for storage and display in the town's Castle.

Disappearance and Mystery

Later in the war, Königsberg was heavily bombarded by the Royal Air Force, then further very heavily damaged by the advancing Soviets before and after its fall on April 9, 1945. The Amber Room was never seen again, though reports have occasionally surfaced stating that components of the Amber Room survived the war.

There have been numerous conflicting reports and theories, among them that the Amber Room was destroyed by bombing, hidden in a now-lost subterranean bunker in Königsberg, buried in mines in a mountain range on the Czech / Polish – German border not far from Berlin, or taken onto a Nazi ship or submarine which was sunk by Soviet forces in the Baltic Sea.

Many different individuals and groups, including a number of different entities from the government of the Soviet Union, have mounted extensive searches for it at various times since the war, with little result. At one point in 1998, two separate teams (one in Germany, the other in Lithuania) announced that they had located the Amber Room, the first in a silver mine, the second buried in a lagoon; neither produced the Amber Room.

However, in 1997 one Italian stone mosaic that was part of a set of four which had decorated the Amber Room did turn up in West Germany, in the possession of the family of a soldier who had helped pack up the Amber Room.

Destruction Theory

Recently, a pair of British investigative journalists conducted lengthy research on the fate of the Amber Room, including extensive archival research in Russia. In 2004, their book concluded that the Amber Room was most likely destroyed when Königsberg Castle was burned out, shortly after Königsberg surrendered to occupying Soviet forces.

Documents from the archives showed that that was also the conclusion of the report of Alexander Brusov, chief of the first formal mission sent by the Soviet government to find the Amber Room, who wrote in June, 1945: 'Summarising all the facts, we can say that the Amber Room was destroyed between 9 and 11 April, 1945'. Some years later, Brusov later gave a contrary opinion; the book authors intimate that this change of opinion was likely due to pressure from other Soviet officials, who did not want to be seen as responsible for the loss of the Amber Room.

Among other information from the archives was the revelation that the remains of the rest of the set of Italian stone mosaics were found in the burned debris of the castle. The authors' reasoning as to why the Soviets conducted extensive searches for the Amber Room in the years after WWII, even though their own experts had concluded that it was destroyed, is that it served the differing motives of several elements in the Soviet government: some wished to obscure (even from other branches of the Soviet government) the fact that Soviet soldiers may have been responsible for its destruction; others found the theft of the Amber Room a useful Cold War propaganda tool, and did not want to lose a valuable 'talking point'; still others did not want to share the blame for its destruction (through their failure to evacuate the Amber Room to safety at the start of the war).

Russian officials have denied the book's conclusions. Said Adelaida Yolkina, senior researcher at the Pavlovsk Museum Estate: 'It is impossible to see the Red Army being so careless that they let the Amber Room be destroyed.' Other Russian experts were less sceptical, and had a different point to make; Mikhail Piotrovsky, director of the State Hermitage Museum, was very cautious in his comments, and said: 'Most importantly, the destruction of the Amber Room during the Second World War is fault of the people who started the war.' In reply, Catherine Scott-Clark, one of the authors, indicated that they only came to their conclusions with reluctance: 'When we started working on this issue, we were hoping to be able to find the Amber Room.'

Since the book came out, a Russian veteran has given an interview in which he confirmed their basic conclusion as to the fate of the Amber Room, although he denies that the fires were deliberate. 'I probably was one of the last people who saw the Amber Room', said Leonid Arinshtein, a literature expert with the nongovernmental Russian Culture Foundation, who was a Red Army lieutenant in charge of a rifle platoon in Königsberg in 1945. 'The Red Army didn't burn anything,' he said.

A variation of this theory is common currency amongst present-day residents of Kaliningrad. This is that part at least of the room was found in the cellars after WWII by the Red Army, in relatively good condition. This was not admitted at the time in order to keep blame on the Germans. To preserve this story access to the ruins of the castle, which were still pretty substantial after WWII, was restricted, even to historical/archaeological surveys. During the 1960s, access to the site was suddenly withheld and the ruins were blown up by the Army, sealing any access to the underground area. The still uncompleted Dom Sovietov was built over the central area. The remains of the room may still be sited underground; however, as mentioned above, amber which is not cared for will crumble into dust. It is presumed that this is what has happened and that the Russian authorities, even after Communism, have been unwilling to admit this.

In 1979, a reconstruction effort began at Tsarskoye Selo, based largely on black and white photographs of the original Amber Room.

Financial difficulties were helped with money donated by a German company. By 2003, the titanic work of the Russian craftsmen was mostly completed. The new room was dedicated by Russian President Vladimir Putin and German Chancellor Gerhard Schröder at the 300-year anniversary of the city of Saint Petersburg.

In Kleinmachnow, near Berlin, there is a miniature Amber Room, fabricated after the original. The Berlin miniature collector Ulla Klingbeil had this copy made of original East Prussian amber. The exhibit fee at Europarc Dreilinden is donated to the Arilex-Verein Foundation to aid handicapped children.

In 1991, during a visit to Germany, Russian president Boris Yeltsin demanded the return of the Amber Room, apparently believing that it still lay hidden somewhere within Germanys borders.

Priam's Treasure – The Treasures of Troy

Priam's Treasure is a cache of gold and other artefacts discovered by classical archaeologist Heinrich Schliemann. Schliemann claimed the site to be that of ancient Troy, and assigned the artefacts to the Homeric king Priam. This assignment is now thought to be a result of Schliemann's zeal to find sites and objects mentioned in the Homeric epics. At the time the stratigraphy at Troy had not been solidified, which was done subsequently by the archaeologist Carl Blegen. The layer in which Priam's Treasure was alleged to have been found was assigned to Troy II, whereas Priam would have been king of Troy VI or VIIa, occupied hundreds of years later.

Background

With the rise of modern critical history, Troy and the Trojan War were consigned to the realms of legend. In 1871-73 and 1878-79, Schliemann excavated a hill called Hissarlik in the Ottoman Empire, near the town of Chanak (Çanakkale) in north-western Anatolia. Here, he discovered the ruins of a series of ancient cities, dating from the Bronze Age to the Roman period. Schliemann declared one of these cities – at first Troy I, later Troy II – to be the city of Troy, and this identification was widely accepted at that time.

Concerning events on or about May 27, 1873 Schliemann reported:

In excavating this wall further and directly by the side of the palace of King Priam, I came upon a large copper article of the most remarkable form, which attracted my attention all the more as I thought I saw gold behind it. In order to withdraw the treasure from the greed of my workmen, and to save it for archaeology, I immediately had "paidos" (lunch break) called. While the men were eating and resting, I cut out the Treasure with a large knife. It would, however, have been impossible for me to have removed the Treasure without the help of my dear wife, who stood by me ready to pack the things which I cut out in her shawl and to carry them away.

Schliemann's oft-repeated story of the treasure being carried by his wife, Sophie, in her shawl was untrue. Schliemann later admitted making it up, saying that at the time of the discovery, Sophie was in

Priam's Treasure

fact with her family in Athens, following the death of her father.

The Treasure

A partial catalogue of the treasure is approximately as follows:

- A copper shield;
- A copper cauldron with handles;
- An unknown copper artefact, perhaps the hasp of a chest;
- A silver vase containing two gold diadems (the "Jewels of Helen"), 8750 gold rings, buttons and other small objects, six gold bracelets, two gold goblets;
- A copper vase ;
- A wrought gold bottle;
- Two gold cups, one wrought, one cast;
- A number of red terra cotta goblets;
- An electrum cup (mixture of gold and silver and copper);
- Six wrought silver knife blades (which Schliemann put forward as money);
- Three silver vases with fused copper parts;
- More silver goblets and vases;
- Thirteen copper lance heads;
- Fourteen copper axes;
- Seven copper daggers;
- Other copper artefacts with the key to a chest.

The Treasure as an Art Collection

Apparently, Schliemann smuggled Priam's Treasure out of Anatolia. The officials were informed when his wife, Sophia, wore the jewels for the public. The Ottoman official assigned to watch the excavation, Amin Effendi, received a prison sentence. The Ottoman government revoked Schliemann's permission to dig and sued him for its share of the gold. Schliemann went on to Mycenae. There, however, the Greek Archaeological Society sent an agent to monitor him.

Later Schliemann traded some treasure to the government of the Ottoman Empire in exchange for permission to dig at Troy again. It is located in the Istanbul Archaeology Museum. The rest was acquired in 1881 by the Royal Museums of Berlin (Königliche Museen zu Berlin), in whose hands it remained until 1945, when it disappeared from a protective bunker beneath the Berlin Zoo.

In fact, the treasure had been removed to the Soviet Union by the Red Army. During the Cold War, the government of the Soviet Union denied any knowledge of the fate of Priam's Treasure. However, in September 1993 the treasure turned up at the Pushkin Museum in Moscow. The return of items taken from museums has been arranged in a treaty with Germany but, as of January 2010, is being blocked by museum directors in Russia. They are keeping the looted art, they say, as compensation for the destruction of Russian cities and looting of Russian museums by Nazi Germany in World War II.

Authenticity of the Treasure

There have always been doubts about the authenticity of the treasure. Within the last few decades these doubts have found fuller expression in articles and books.

The World War I Romanian Treasure

The Romanian Treasure is a collection of valuable objects the Romanian government sent to Russia for safekeeping during World War I. It was only partially returned as of 2010.

Historical Background

During World War I, since Bucharest was occupied by Germany, the Romanian administration moved to Iasi, and with them, the most valuable objects which belonged to the Romanian state. Fearing an eventual German victory, the Romanian government decided to send the Treasure abroad.

Among the ideas considered was to send it for safekeeping to the vaults of the Bank of England or even to send it to the United States, but there was the problem of transportation, since Germany and its allies controlled most of Central Europe and sending it via Northern Europe was dangerous, as the Germans could have intercepted it.

The decision had to be taken by the Romanian Prime Minister Ion I. C. Bratianu. Although the banker Mauriciu Blank advised him to send it to London or to a neutral country, such as Denmark, Bratianu feared the German submarines of the North Sea and chose another ally of Romania in World War I, Russia, using the argument that "Russia would feel offended if they sent it to England".

During World War II, the valuables of the National Bank of Romania were not taken outside of Romania, but hidden inside a cave near Tismana, Gorj County and from there, they were safely recovered after the war.

Sending the Treasure

The Romanian government signed a deal with the Russian government which stated that Russia would safekeep the Romanian Treasure in the Kremlin until the end of the war.

At 3:00 a.m. during the night of December 14-15, 1916, a train with 17 carriages, full of gold bars and gold coins (around 97 tonnes), departed the Iaşi train station eastward. In four other carriages, two hundred gendarmes guarded the train. The gold load of this train has as of 2005 a value of $1.25 billion.

Seven months later, in the summer of 1917, as the war situation was getting worse for Romania, another transport was sent to Moscow, containing the most precious objects of the Romanian state, including the archives of the Romanian Academy, many antique valuables, such as 3,500-year-old golden jewels found in Romania, ancient Dacian jewels, the jewels of the voivodes of Wallachia and Moldavia, as well as the jewels of the Romanian royalty, thousands of paintings, as well as precious cult objects owned by Romanian monasteries, such as 14th century icons and old Romanian manuscripts. It also contained various deposits of the Romanian people at the national banks. The value of this train is hard to estimate, especially because most of its contents are art objects, but most likely nowadays it could even surpass the value of the other train.

Soviet Russia and Soviet Union

After the Romanian Army entered Bessarabia, at the time nominally part of Russia, in the early 1918, the new Soviet government severed all diplomatic relations and confiscated the Romanian treasure. The Romanian government tried to recover the treasure in 1922, but with little success. In 1935, the USSR did return a part of the archives, and in 1956 paintings and ancient objects, most notably, the Pietroasele treasure. The most important and valuable part (about 40 of the 42 carriages), however, was never returned.

All the governments of Romania since World War I, regardless of their political colour, have tried unsuccessfully to negotiate a return of the gold and of the culturally valuable objects, but all Soviet and Russian governments have refused. The Soviet Union tried to use the treasure in the dispute over Bessarabia, however no agreement was reached.

The Treasure since 1917

Very little is known about the Treasure after the October Revolution, but it appears that during World War II all the valuables held by the Soviet state (and presumably of the Romanian state) were taken out from Moscow and sent toward the regions which were 'not endangered'. However, it is clear that they were not kept sealed, as the agreement with the Romanian government said, as the chests of the archives which were returned in 1935 had obviously been rummaged through and many objects and documents were missing.

Recent Negotiations

After the fall of the USSR, the Russian governments' position toward the Romanian Treasure remained the same and various negotiations failed. The Romanian-Russian treaty of 2003 did not mention the Treasure; Presidents Ion Iliescu and Vladimir Putin decided to create a commission to analyse this problem, but no advances were made.

The Search for Lost Legendary Treasures

The Treasure of Rennes-le-Chateau

Rennes-le-Château is a medieval castle village and a commune in the Aude département, in the Languedoc area in southern France, an area known for its towering mountains, deep gorges, forests, caves, wild remote plateaus and access to the Mediterranean.

History of the Village

This predominantly rural area has a very rich history, as evidenced by its castles, cathedrals, vineyards and museums. Mountains frame both ends of the region – the Cevennes to the northeast and the Pyrenees to the south. Jagged ridges, deep river canyons and rocky limestone plateaus, with vast caves beneath, make it one of the most scenic spots on earth.

Over the centuries religious and political conflicts have caused much havoc in the area. The ruined castles which cling precariously to hilltops played a leading role in the struggles between the Catholic church and the Cathars at the beginning of the 13th century. Others guarded the volatile border with Spain. Whole communities were wiped out during the campaigns of the Catholic authorities to rid the area of the Cathar heretics during the Albigensian Crusades and later, when Protestants fought for religious freedom against the French monarchy.

Modern Fame

The modern reputation of Rennes-le-Château rises from rumours dating from the mid-1950s and not from the lifetime of a local nineteenth century priest Bérenger Saunière, who was alleged to have mysteriously acquired and spent large sums of money (despite the existence of much evidence proving the contrary). Published by French Editions Belisane from the early 1980s onwards, the evidence ranged from the archives in the possession of Antoine Captier, which includes Saunière's correspondence and notebooks, and the minutes of the ecumenical trial between Saunière and his bishop between 1910-1911 which are located in the Carcassonne Bishopric. All of the evidence demonstrates that Saunière's source of wealth lay in the trafficking of masses: this is not 'opinion', but historical fact, emphasised by French authors like Rene Descadeillas and Jean-Jacques Bedu. He was even said to have visited several heads of state, though there is no evidence for this whatsoever. These rumours were given wide local circulation in the 1950s by Noel Corbu, a local man who had opened a restaurant in Saunière's former estate who probably hoped to attract business. They moved from local to national importance when they were incorporated by Pierre Plantard into his mythology of the Priory of Sion, which influenced the authors of the popular 1982 book *The Holy Blood and the Holy Grail*.

From this point on Rennes-le-Château became the centre of conspiracy theories claiming that Saunière uncovered hidden treasure and/or secrets about the history of the Church that threatened the foundations of Catholicism. Since the mid-1950s, the area has become the focus of increasingly sensational claims involving the Knights Templar, the Priory of Sion, the Rex Deus, the Holy Grail, the treasures of the Temple of Solomon, the Ark of the Covenant, ley lines, geometric alignments, and others. Elements of these ideas were later incorporated into Umberto Eco's 1989 novel *Foucault's Pendulum*, Michael Baigent's, Henry Lincoln's and Richard

Rennes-le-Chateau

Leigh's bestselling *The Holy Blood and the Holy Grail*, Dan Brown's bestselling 2003 novel *The Da Vinci Code* (which borrows heavily from *The Holy Blood and the Holy Grail*), and the computer game *Gabriel Knight III*.

The village now attracts visitors who look for hidden treasures and evidence of conspiracy, much to the displeasure of the locals.

Sceptical Views

Almost all historians reject these conspiracies as nothing more than fantasy. According to writers such as Paul Smith, Monsignor George Boyer in 1967 (Vicar General of the parish of Carcassonne), Rene Descadeillas, Jacques Rivière, Jean-Luc Chaumeil, Jean-Jacques Bedu, Vincianne Denis, Bill Putnam, John Edwin Wood, and Marie Francine Etchegoin – the stories of Saunière's 'mysteries' were based on nothing more than a minor scandal involving the sale of masses, which eventually led to the disgrace of both Saunière and his bishop. His 'wealth' was short-lived and he died relatively poor. Other aspects of the Rennes-le-Château legend derive from forgeries created on behalf of Pierre Plantard.

Lost City of Gold – El Dorado

El Dorado Spanish for "the golden one" is the name of a Muisca tribal chief who covered himself with gold dust and, as an initiation rite, dived into a highland lake.

Later it became the name of a legendary "Lost City of Gold" that has fascinated – and so far eluded – explorers since the days of the Spanish Conquistadors. Though many have searched for years on end to find this city of gold, no evidence of such a place has been found.

Imagined as a place, El Dorado became a kingdom, an empire, the city of this legendary golden king. In pursuit of the legend, Francisco Orellana and Gonzalo Pizarro would depart from Quito in 1541 in a famous and disastrous expedition towards the Amazon Basin; as a result of this, however, Orellana became the first person known to navigate the Amazon River all the way to its mouth.

Tribal Ceremony

The original narrative is to be found in the rambling chronicle, El Carnero, of Juan Rodriguez Freyle. According to Freyle, the king or chief priest of the Muisca was said to be ritually covered with gold dust at a religious festival held in Lake Guatavita, near present-day Bogotá Colombia.

In 1638, Juan Rodriguez Troxell wrote this account, addressed to the cacique or governor of Guatavita:

"The ceremony took place on the appointment of a new ruler. Before taking office, he spent some time secluded in a cave, without women, forbidden to eat salt, or to go out during daylight. The first journey he had to make was to go to the great lagoon of Guatavita, to make offerings and sacrifices to the demon which they worshipped as their God and lord. During the ceremony, which took place at the lagoon, they made a raft of rushes, embellishing and decorating it with the most attractive things they had. They put on it four lighted braziers in which they burned much moque, which is the incense of these natives, and also resin and many other perfumes. The lagoon was large and deep, so that a ship with high sides could sail on it, all loaded with an infinity of men and women dressed in fine plumes, golden plaques and crowns. As soon as those on the raft began to burn incense, they also lit braziers on the shore, so that the smoke hid the light of day. At this time they stripped the heir to his skin, and anointed him with a sticky earth on which they placed gold dust so that he was completely covered with this metal. They placed him on the raft and at his feet they placed a great heap of gold and emeralds for him to offer to his God. In the raft with him went four principal subject chiefs, decked in plumes, crowns, bracelets, pendants and ear rings all of gold. They, too, were naked, and each one carried his offering .... when the raft reached the centre of the lagoon, they raised a banner as a signal for silence. The gilded Indian then threw out all the pile of gold into the middle of the lake, and the chiefs who had accompanied him did the same on their own accounts. After this they lowered the flag, which had remained up during the whole time of offering, and, as the raft moved towards the shore, the shouting began again, with pipes, flutes, and large teams of singers and dancers. With this ceremony the new ruler was received, and was recognised as lord and king."

The Muisca towns and their treasures quickly fell to the conquistadores. Taking stock of their newly-won territory, the Spaniards realised that – in spite of the quantity of gold in the hands of the Indians – there were no golden cities, nor even rich mines, since the Muiscas obtained all their gold in trade. But at the same time, the Spanish began to hear stories of El Dorado from captured Indians, and of the rites which used to take place at the lagoon of Guatavita.

Expeditions

El Dorado is applied to a legendary story in which precious stones were found in fabulous abundance along with gold coins. The concept of El Dorado underwent several transformations, and eventually accounts of the previous myth were also combined with those of the legendary city. The resulting El Dorado enticed European explorers for two centuries.

Among the earliest stories was the one told by Diego de Ordaz's lieutenant Martinez, who claimed to have been rescued from shipwreck, conveyed inland, and entertained by El Dorado himself (1531).

In 1540, Gonzalo Pizarro, the younger half-brother of Francisco Pizarro, was made the governor of the provenance of Quito in northern Ecuador. Shortly after taking lead in Quito, Gonzalo learned from many of the natives of a valley far to the east rich in both cinnamon and gold. He banded together 340 soldiers and about 4000 natives in 1541 and led them eastward down the Rio Coca and Rio Napo. Francisco de Orellana, Gonzalo's nephew, accompanied his uncle on this expedition. Gonzalo quit after many of the soldiers and natives had died from hunger, disease, and periodic attacks by hostile natives. He ordered Orellana to continue downstream, where he eventually made it to the Atlantic Ocean, discovering the Amazon (named Amazon because of a tribe of female warriors that attacked Orellana's men while on their voyage.)

Other expeditions include that of Philipp von Hutten (1541-1545), who led an exploring party from Coro on the coast of Venezuela; and of Gonzalo Jiménez de Quesada, the Governor of El Dorado, who started from Bogotá (1569).

Sir Walter Raleigh, who resumed the search in 1595, described El Dorado as a city on Lake Parime far up the Orinoco River in Guyana. This city on the lake was marked on English and other maps until its existence was disproved by Alexander von Humboldt during his Latin-America expedition (1799-1804).

Metaphor

In the mythology of the Muisca today, gold (Mnya) represents the energy contained in the trinity of Chiminigagua, which constitutes the creative power of everything that exists. Chiminigagua is, along with Bachué, Cuza, Chibchachum, Bochica, and Nemcatacoa, one of the creators of the universe.

Meanwhile, the name of El Dorado came to be used metaphorically of any place where wealth could be rapidly acquired. It was given to El Dorado County, California, and to towns and cities in various states. It has also been anglicized to the single word Eldorado.

In literature, frequent allusion is made to the legend, perhaps the best-known references being those in Milton's *Paradise Lost* (Book xi. 408-411) and in Voltaire's *Candide* (chs. 18, 19). *Eldorado* was the title and subject of a four-stanza poem by Edgar Allan Poe. In the

1966, John Wayne film *El Dorado*, most of Poe's poem is recited by the character nicknamed Mississippi and is lyrics in the film's title song. El Dorado is also referenced in Joseph Conrad's novella *Heart of Darkness*. Within Conrad's work, the Eldorado Exploring Expedition journeys into the jungles of Africa in search of conquest and treasure, only to meet an untimely demise.

El Dorado is also sometimes used as a metaphor to represent an ultimate prize or "Holy Grail" that one might spend one's life seeking. It could represent true love, heaven, happiness, or success. It is used sometimes as a figure of speech to represent something much sought after that may not even exist, or, at least, may not ever be found. Such use is evident in Poe's poem *El Dorado*. In this context, El Dorado bears similarity to other myths such as the Fountain of Youth and Shangri-la. The disillusionment side of the ideal quest metaphor may be represented by Helldorado, a satirical nickname given to Tombstone by a tardy miner who complained that many of his profession had travelled far to find El Dorado, only to wind up washing dishes in restaurants.

Werner Herzog's film, Aguirre, the Wrath of God, also explores the El Dorado metaphor. The main character, Lope de Aguirre, is historically based, but is actually an amalgam of Aguirre and Francisco Orellana.

Lost Treasures of Quivira

Quivira is a place first mentioned by Francisco Vazquez de Coronado in 1541, who visited it during his searches for the mythical "Seven Cities of Gold". The location and identity of the "Quivirans" has been much debated over a wide area, including Kansas, Nebraska, and Missouri. They are most often considered to have been Wichita or another Caddoan tribe (Pawnee, Arikara, etc.).

Discovery

In 1539, the Spaniard Francisco Vasquez de Coronado led a large expedition north from Mexico to search for wealth and the "Seven Cities of Cibola". Instead of wealth, he found farming peoples living in the flat-roofed adobe towns in what are today Arizona and New Mexico. These were the Hopi, Zuni, and Rio Grande Pueblo Indians of today. Coronado was disappointed by the lack of wealth among the Pueblos, but he heard from an Indian the Spanish called "the Turk" of a wealthy civilisation named Quivira far to the east, where the chief supposedly drank from golden cups hanging from the trees. Following this tale he led his army of more than one thousand Spaniards and Indian allies onto the Great Plains. The Turk was to guide him to Quivira.

Coronado traversed the panhandle of Texas in 1541. He found two groups of Indians, the Querechos and the Teyas. He was heading southeast when the Teyas told him that the Turk was taking him the wrong direction and that Quivira was to the north. It appears the Turk was luring the Spaniards away from New Mexico with tales of wealth in Quivira, hoping perhaps that they would get lost in the vastness of the Plains. Coronado sent most of his slow-moving army back to New Mexico. With 30 mounted Spaniards, priests and Indian followers, the Turk, and Teya guides he forced into service, he set off northward to Quivira. After a march of more than thirty days, he found a large

In search of lost treasure of Quivira

river, probably the Arkansas, and soon met several Indians hunting buffalo. They led him to Quivira.

Description of Quivira

Coronado found Quivira well settled. The land itself being very fat and black and being very well watered by the rivulets and springs and rivers. He found prunes like those of Spain, and nuts and very good sweet grapes and mulberries. It was, he said, the best land he had seen in his long trek. He spent 25 days in Quivira and travelled about 65 miles (25 leagues) from one end of the country to the other. He found nothing more than straw-thatched villages of up to two hundred houses each and fields of corn, beans, and squash. He found no gold, other than a single small piece which he reasoned had come into the natives' hands from a member of his own expedition.

The Quivirans were simple people. Both men and women were nearly naked. They were large people of good build, many of the men being over six feet tall. They seemed like giants compared to the Spaniards.

Coronado was escorted to the further edge of Quivira, called Tabas, where the neighbouring land of Harahey began. He summoned the "Lord of Harahey" and he with two hundred followers came to meet the Spanish. The Harahey Indians were all naked – with bows and some sort of things on their heads, and their privy parts slightly covered. It was the same sort of place and of about the same size as Quivira. Disappointed at his failure to find wealth, Coronado turned his face toward New Mexico and marched back across the plains, met up with the rest of the army there, and the following year returned to Mexico. Before leaving Quivira, Coronado ordered that the Turk be strangled. The Coronado expedition had failed in its quest for gold.

Coronado left behind in New Mexico several Catholic priests and their helpers, including Friar Juan de Padilla. Padilla journeyed back to Quivira with a Portuguese assistant and several Christian Indians. The friar and most of his companions were soon killed by the Quivirians, apparently because he wished to leave their country to visit their enemies, the Guas. The Portuguese and one Indian survived to tell the story.

Later Expeditions to Quivira

In 1594, Francisco Leyba (Leyva) Bonilla and Antonio de Humana (Umana) made another attempt to find the Quivira of Coronado, even though it was denounced as unauthorised by Spanish officials. Only one Mexican Indian, Jusepe Gutierrez returned from this journey. He related that Leyba had killed Umana in a quarrel and that he had deserted the expedition.

Following this, in 1601, the governor of New Mexico, Don Juan de Oñate, made another expedition in search of Quivira. He found settlements of the Escanjaque and Rayado Indians in Kansas or Oklahoma, but no gold or silver. He learned that the Leyba and other members of the Umana and Lebya expedition had been killed by Indians. In 1606, 800 of these "Quivirans" were said to have visited Oñate in New Mexico.

Quivira is again mentioned in a 1634 expedition of Captain Alonzo Vaca who found it 300 leagues east of New Mexico. Another expedition was made in 1662 by Diego Dionisio de Penalosa, who allegedly found a large settlement he called a city, but a 1919 study claimed this account to have been spurious. The enemies of the Quivirans in all these accounts were the Escanjaques. In 1675 and 1678 came "two Spanish royal orders for the conquest of Quivira".

Where was Quivira and Who were the Quivirans?

Archaeological evidence has suggested that Quivira was located near the Great Bend of the Arkansas River in central Kansas. The remains of several Indian settlements have been found near Lyons along Cow Creek and the Little Arkansas River along with articles of Spanish manufacture dating from Coronado's time.

The Quivirans were almost certainly the Indians who came later to be called the Wichita. Coronado's meagre descriptions of Quivira resemble the Wichita villages of historic times. The Quivirans seem to have been numerous, based on the number of settlements Coronado visited, with a population of at least 10,000 persons. They were good farmers as well as buffalo hunters. Judging from Coronado's description they were a healthy and peaceful people.

The province of Harahey Coronado found on the borders of Quivira may have been located on the Smoky Hill River near the present city of Salina, Kansas. The people of Harahey were probably Pawnee, a tribe related by language and culture to the Wichita.

The first European definitively known to visit the Great Bend region after Coronado was the French explorer Etienne de Bourgmont. In 1724, Bourgmont journeyed with an escort of Kaw and other Indians westward from the Missouri River to a large village of Indians believed to be Apaches. The village was near Lyons, precisely where Quivira had been almost 200 years earlier.

It has been suggested that the original Quivirans had moved to eastern Kansas and south to Oklahoma. Their reasons for moving may have been to escape the depredations of the Apache, aggressive newcomers to the Great Plains. It also appears that the Wichita of the 18th century were fewer in number than the Quivirans of the 16th century. It is probable that smallpox and other diseases introduced by Europeans took their toll on the Quivirans as they did on many of the Indian tribes in the Americans.

The origin of the word "Quivira" is uncertain. It is possible that the inhabitants of Coronado's Quivira called themselves Tancoa and Tabas. These two names are similar to later Wichita sub-tribes called Tawakonis and Taovayas.

Quivira in Cartography

On early 16th and 17th century maps of North America, a large region including what is now Kansas, Oklahoma, southeastern Colorado, northeastern New Mexico and the Texas panhandle was called Quivira.

The last remnants of the formerly extensive cartographic region of "Quivira" today is the city of Lake Quivira and the Quivira National Wildlife Refuge in Kansas. In addition, there is the "Quivira Council" of the Boy Scouts, serving the area of southwestern Kansas around Wichita, Kansas, the central part of the area that was traditionally called Quivira. There is also a major arterial in the Kansas suburbs of Kansas City named "Quivira Road".

An abandoned Indian Pueblo in Torrance County, New Mexico has been given the name La Gran Quivira (The Great Quivira). The site was inhabited during the early period of Spanish occupation, when the settlement was called Pueblo de Las Humanas. The remains of La Gran Quivira settlement are today part of Salinas Pueblo Missions National Monument.

Tomb of King Tutankhamun

Though several of the foremost excavators over the past century had declared that there was nothing left to find in the Valley of the Kings, Howard Carter and his sponsor, Lord Carnarvon, spent a number of years and a lot of money searching for a tomb for which they weren't sure whether it existed or not. In November 1922, they found it. Carter had discovered not just an unknown ancient Egyptian tomb, but one that had lain nearly undisturbed for over 3,000 years. What lay within astounded the world.

The Long Search

Howard Carter had worked in Egypt for 31 years before he found King Tut's tomb. Carter had begun his career in Egypt at age 17, using his artistic talents to copy wall scenes and inscriptions. Only eight years later (in 1899), Carter was appointed the Inspector-General of Monuments in Upper Egypt. In 1905, Carter resigned from this job and in 1907, Carter went to work for Lord Carnarvon.

George Edward Stanhope Molyneux Herbert, the fifth Earl of Carnarvon, loved to race around in the newly-invented of the automobile. Enjoying the speed his automobile afforded, Lord Carnarvon had an auto accident in 1901 which left him in ill health. Vulnerable to the damp English winter, Lord Carnarvon began spending winters in Egypt in 1903 and to pass the time, he took up archaeology as a hobby. Turning up nothing but a mummified cat (still in its coffin) his first season, Lord Carnarvon decided to hire someone knowledgeable for the succeeding seasons. For this, he hired Howard Carter.

Tomb of Tutankhamun

After several relatively successful seasons working together, World War I brought a near halt to their work in Egypt. Yet, by the fall of 1917, Carter and his sponsor, Lord Carnarvon, began excavating in earnest in the Valley of the Kings.

Carter stated that there were several pieces of evidence – a faience cup, a piece of gold foil, and a cache of funerary items which all bore the name of Tutankhamun – already found that convinced him that the tomb of King Tut had not yet been found. Carter also believed that the locations of these items pointed to a specific area where they might find King Tutankhamun's tomb. Carter was determined to systematically search this area by excavating down to the bedrock.

Besides some ancient workmen's huts at the foot of the tomb of Rameses VI and 13 calcite jars at the entrance to the tomb of Merenptah, Carter did not have much to show after five years of excavating in the Valley of the Kings. Thus, Lord Carnarvon made the decision to stop the search. After a discussion with Carter, Carnarvon relented and agreed to one last season.

By November 1, 1922, Carter began his final season working in the Valley of the Kings by having his workers expose the workmen's huts at the base of the tomb of Rameses VI. After exposing and documenting the huts, Carter and his workmen began to excavate the ground beneath them.

By the fourth day of work, they had found something – a step that had been cut into the rock.

Uncertainty

Work continued feverishly on the afternoon of November 4th through the following morning. By late afternoon, on November 5th, 12 stairs (leading downwards) were revealed; and in front of them, stood the upper portion of a blocked entrance. Carter searched the plastered door for a name but of the seals that could be read, he found only the impıessions of the royal necropolis. Carter was extremely excited:

"The design was certainly of the Eighteenth Dynasty. Could it be the tomb of a noble buried here by royal consent? Was it a royal cache, a hiding-place to which a mummy and its equipment had been removed for safety? Or was it actually the tomb of the king for whom I had spent so many years in search?"

To protect the find, Carter had his workmen fill in the stairs, covering them so that none were showing. While several of Carter's most trusted workmen stood guard, Carter left to make preparations. The first of which was contacting Lord Carnarvon in England to share the news of the find. On November 6th, two days after finding the first step, Carter sent a cable: "At last have made wonderful discovery in Valley; a magnificent tomb with seals intact; re-covered same for your arrival; congratulations."

It was nearly three weeks after finding the first step that Carter was able to proceed. On November 23rd, Lord Carnarvon and his daughter, Lady Evelyn Herbert, arrived in Luxor. The following day, the workers had again cleared the staircase, now exposing all 16 of its steps and the full face of the sealed doorway. Now Carter found what he could not see before, since the bottom of the doorway had still been covered with rubble – there were several seals on the bottom of the door with Tutankhamun's name on them.

Now that the door was fully exposed, they also noticed that the upper left of the doorway had been broken through, presumably by tomb robbers, and resealed. The tomb was not intact; yet the fact that the tomb had been resealed showed that the tomb had not been emptied.

On the morning of November 25th, the sealed doorway was photographed and the seals noted. Then the door was removed. A passageway emerged from the darkness, filled to the top with limestone chips. Upon closer examination, Carter could tell that tomb robbers had dug a hole through the upper left section of the passageway (the hole had been refilled in antiquity with larger, darker rocks than used for the rest of the fill).

This meant that the tomb had probably been raided twice in antiquity. The first time was within a few years of the king's burial and before there was a sealed door and fill in the passageway (scattered objects were found under the fill). The second time, the robbers had to dig through the fill and could only escape with smaller items.

By the following afternoon, the fill along the 26-foot-long passageway had been cleared away to expose another sealed door, almost identical to the first. Again, there were signs that a hole had been made in the doorway and resealed.

"We were firmly convinced by this time that it was a cache that we were about to open, and not a tomb. The arrangement of stairway, entrance passage and doors reminded us forcibly of the cache of Akhenaten and

Tyi material found in the very near vicinity of the present excavation by Davis, and the fact that Tutankhamun's seals occurred there likewise seemed almost certain proof that we were right in our conjecture. We were soon to know. There lay the sealed doorway, and behind it was the answer to the question."

Wonderful Things

Tension mounted. If there was anything left inside, it would be a discovery of a lifetime for Carter. If the tomb was relatively intact, it would be something the world had never seen.

"With trembling hands I made a tiny breach in the upper left-hand corner. Darkness and blank space, as far as an iron testing-rod could reach, showed that whatever lay beyond was empty, and not filled like the passage we had just cleared. Candle tests were applied as a precaution against possible foul gases, and then, widening the hold a little, I inserted the candle and peered in, Lord Carnarvon, Lady Evelyn and Callender standing anxiously beside me to hear the verdict. At first I could see nothing, the hot air escaping from the chamber causing the candle flame to flicker, but presently, as my eyes grew accustomed to the light, details of the room within emerged slowly from the mist, strange animals, statues, and gold – everywhere the glint of gold. For the moment – an eternity it must have seemed to the others standing by – I was struck dumb with amazement, and when Lord Carnarvon, unable to stand the suspense any longer, inquired anxiously, "Can you see anything?" it was all I could do to get out the words, "Yes, wonderful things."

The next morning, the plastered door was photographed and the seals documented. Then the door came down, revealing the Antechamber. The wall opposite the entrance wall was piled nearly to the ceiling with boxes, chairs, couches, and so much more – most of them gold – in an "organised chaos".

On the right wall stood two life-size statues of the king, facing each other as if to protect the sealed entrance that was between them. This sealed door also showed signs of being broken into and resealed, but this time the robbers had entered in the bottom middle of the door.

To the left of the door from the passageway lay a tangle of parts from several dismantled chariots.

As Carter and the others spent time looking at the room and its contents, they noticed another sealed door behind the couches on the far wall. This sealed door also had a hole in it, but unlike the others, the hole had not been resealed. Carefully, they crawled under the couch and shone their light.

In this room (later called the Annexe) everything was in disarray. Carter theorised that officials had attempted to straighten up the Antechamber after the robbers had plundered, but they had made no attempt to straighten the Annexe.

"I think the discovery of this second chamber, with its crowded contents, had a somewhat sobering effect on us. Excitement had gripped us hitherto, and given us no pause for thought, but now for the first time we began to realise what a prodigious task we had in front of us, and what a responsibility it entailed. This was no ordinary find, to be disposed of in a normal season's work; nor was there any precedent to show us how to handle it. The thing was outside all experience, bewildering, and for the moment it seemed as though there were more to be done than any human agency could accomplish."

Be Careful!

Before the entrance between the two statues in the Antechamber could be opened, the items in the Antechamber needed to be removed or risk damage to them from flying debris, dust, and movement. Documentation and preservation of each item was a monumental task. Carter realised that this project was larger than he could handle alone, thus he asked for, and received, help from a large number of specialists.

To begin the clearing process, each item was photographed in situ, both with an assigned number and without. Then, a sketch and description of each item was made on correspondingly number record cards. Next, the item was noted on a ground plan of the tomb (only for the Antechamber).

Carter and his team had to be extremely careful when attempting to remove any of the objects. Since many of the items were in extremely delicate states (such as beaded sandals in which the threading had disintegrated, leaving only beads held together by 3,000 years of habit), many items needed immediate treatment, such as a celluloid spray, to keep the items intact for removal. Moving the items also proved a challenge.

"Clearing the objects from the Antechamber was like playing a gigantic game of spillikins. So crowded were they that it was a matter of extreme difficulty to move one without running serious risk of damaging others, and in some cases they were so inextricably tangled that an elaborate system of props and supports had to be devised to hold one object or group of objects in place while another was being removed. At such times life was a nightmare."

When an item was successfully removed, it was placed upon a stretcher and gauze and other bandages were wrapped around the item to protect it for removal. Once a number of stretchers were filled, a team of people would carefully pick them up and move them out of the tomb.

As soon as they exited the tomb with the stretchers, they were greeted by hundreds of tourists and reporters who waited for them at the top. Since word had spread quickly around the world about the tomb, the popularity of the site was excessive. Every time someone came out of the tomb, cameras would go off. Owing to remembered images of the recent war, more than one witness thought the items brought bandaged and upon stretchers from the tomb looked like the wounded from World War I. The image must have been especially acute when the life-size statues were removed upon stretchers.

The trail of stretchers were taken to the conservation laboratory, located at some distance away in the tomb of Seti II. Carter had appropriated this tomb to serve as a conservation laboratory, photographic studio, carpenter's shop (to make the boxes needed to ship the objects), and a storeroom. Carter allotted tomb No. 55 as a dark-room.

The items, after conservation and documentation, were very carefully packed into crates and sent by rail to Cairo.

It took Carter and his team seven weeks to clear the Antechamber. On February 17, 1923, they began dismantling the sealed door between the statues.

Burial Chamber

". . . when, after about ten minutes' work, I had made a hole large enough to enable me to do so, I inserted an electric torch. An astonishing sight its light revealed, for there, within a yard of the doorway, stretching as far as one could see and blocking the entrance to the chamber, stood what to all appearances was a solid wall of gold. . . It was, beyond any question, the sepulchral chamber in which we stood, for there, towering above us, was one of the great gilt shrines beneath which kings were laid. So enormous was this structure . . . that it filled within a little the entire area of the chamber, a space of some two feet only separating it from the walls on all four sides, while its roof, with cornice top and torus moulding, reached almost to the ceiling. . ."

The inside of the Burial Chamber was almost completely filled with a large shrine over 16 feet long, 10 feet wide and 9 feet tall. The walls of the shrine were made of gilded wood inlaid with a brilliant blue porcelain.

Unlike the rest of the tomb whose walls had been left as rough-cut rock (unsmoothed and unplastered), the walls of the Burial Chamber (excluding the ceiling) were covered with a gypsum plaster and painted yellow. Upon the yellow walls were painted funerary scenes.

On the ground around the shrine were a number of items, including portions of two broken necklaces that looked as if they had been dropped by robbers and magic oars "to ferry the king's barque (boat) across the waters of the Nether World."

To take apart and examine the shrine, Carter had to first demolish the partition wall between the Antechamber and the Burial Chamber. Still, there was not much room between the three remaining walls and the shrine.

As Carter and his team worked to disassemble the shrine, they found that this was merely the outer shrine, with four shrines in total. Each section of the shrines weighed up to half a ton and in the small confines of the Burial Chamber, work was difficult and uncomfortable.

". . . after our scaffolding and hoisting tackle had been introduced it occupied practically all the available space, leaving little for ourselves in which to work. When some of the parts were freed, there was insufficient room to remove them from the chamber. We bumped our heads, nipped our fingers, we had to squeeze in and out like weasels, and work in all kinds of embarrassing positions."

When the fourth shrine was disassembled, the king's sarcophagus was revealed. The sarcophagus was yellow in colour and made out of a single block of quartzite. The lid did not match the rest of the sarcophagus and had been cracked in the middle during antiquity (an attempt had been made to cover the crack by filling it with gypsum). But what lay underneath?

"The tackle for raising the lid was in position. I gave the word. Amid intense silence the huge slab, broken in two, weighing over a ton and a quarter, rose from its bed. The light shone into the sarcophagus. A sight met our eyes that at first puzzled us. It was a little disappointing. The contents were completely covered by fine linen shrouds. The lid being suspended in mid-air, we rolled back those covering shrouds, one by one, and as the last was removed a gasp of wonderment escaped our lips, so gorgeous was the sight that met our eyes: a golden effigy of the young boy king, of most magnificent workmanship, filled the whole of the interior of the sarcophagus."

A gilded wooden coffin was revealed. The coffin was in a distinctly human shape and was 7 feet 4 inches in length.

A year and a half later, they were ready to lift the lid of the coffin. Conservation work of other objects already removed from the tomb had taken precedence. Thus, the anticipation of what lay beneath was extreme.

When they lifted the lid of the coffin, they found another, smaller coffin. The lifting of the lid of the second coffin revealed a third one, made entirely of gold. On top of this third, and final, coffin was a dark material that had once been liquid and poured over the coffin from the hands to the ankles. The liquid had hardened over the years and firmly stuck the third coffin to the bottom of the second. The thick residue had to be removed with heat and hammering. Then the lid of the third coffin was raised.

"Before us, occupying the whole interior of the golden coffin, was an impressive, neat and carefully made mummy, over which had been poured anointing unguents (ointments) as in the case of the outside of its coffin – again in great quantity – consolidated and blackened by age. In contradistinction to the general dark and sombre effect, due to these unguents, was a brilliant, one might say magnificent, burnished gold mask (picture) or similitude of the king, covering his head and shoulders, which, like the feet, had been intentionally avoided when using the unguents."

At last, the royal mummy of Tutankhamun was revealed. It had been over 3,300 years since a human being had seen the king's remains. This was the first royal Egyptian mummy that had been found untouched since his burial. Carter and the others hoped King Tutankhamun's mummy would reveal a large amount of knowledge about ancient Egyptian burial customs.

Though it was still an unprecedented find, Carter and his team were dismayed to learn that the liquid poured on the mummy had done a great deal of damage. The linen wrappings of the mummy could not be unwrapped as hoped, but instead had to be removed in large chunks. Yet, it was found that the fingers and toes had been wrapped separately.

Unfortunately, many of the items found within the wrappings had also been damaged, many were almost completely disintegrated. Yet, Carter and his team found over 150 items – almost all of them gold – on the mummy, including amulets, bracelets, collars, rings, and daggers.

The autopsy on the mummy found that Tutankhamun had been about 5 feet 5 1/8 inches tall and had died around the age of 18. Certain evidence also attributed Tutankhamun's death to murder.

More Treasure

On the right wall of the Burial Chamber was an entrance into a storeroom, now known as the Treasury. The Treasury, like the Antechamber, was filled with items including many boxes and model boats. Most notable in this room was the large gilded canopic shrine. Inside the gilded shrine was the canopic chest made out of a single block of calcite. Inside the canopic chest were the four canopic jars, each in the shape of an Egyptian coffin and elaborately decorated, holding the pharaoh's embalmed organs – liver, lungs, stomach, and intestines.

Also discovered in the Treasury were two small coffins found in a simple, undecorated wooden box. Inside these two coffins were the mummies of two premature foetuses. It is hypothesised that these were Tutankhamun's children. (Tutankhamun is not known to have had any surviving children.)

World Famous Discovery

The discovery of King Tut's tomb in November 1922 created an obsession around the world. Daily updates of the find were demanded. Masses of mail and telegrams deluged Carter and his associates. Hundreds of tourists waited outside the tomb for a peek.

Hundreds more people tried to use their influential friends and acquaintances to get a tour of the tomb causing a great hindrance to work in the tomb and endangering the artefacts. Ancient Egyptian style clothes quickly hit the markets and appeared in fashion magazines. Even architecture was affected when Egyptian designs were copied into modern buildings.

The rumours and excitement over the discovery became especially acute when Lord Carnarvon became suddenly ill from an infected mosquito bite on his cheek (he had accidentally aggravated it while shaving). On April 5, 1923, within a week of the bite, Lord Carnarvon died. Just as quickly, newspapers were filled with the "news" of a curse.

In all, it took Howard Carter and his colleagues ten years to document and clear out Tutankhamun's tomb. After Carter completed his work at the tomb in 1932, he began to write a six-volume definitive work, *A Report upon the Tomb of Tut'ankh Amun*. Unfortunately, Carter died before he was able to finish. On March 2, 1939, Howard Carter passed away at his home Kensington, London.

The young pharaoh, Tutankhamun, whose own obscurity during his own time allowed his tomb to be forgotten, has now become one of the most well-known pharaohs of ancient Egypt. Having travelled around the world as part of an exhibit, King Tut's body once again rests in his tomb in the Valley of the Kings.

Sree Padmanabhaswamy Temple Treasures

Sree Padmanabhaswamy temple is a Hindu temple dedicated to Lord Vishnu located in Thiruvananthapuram, India. The shrine is currently run by a trust headed by the royal family of Travancore. The temple is one of 108 Divya Desams (Holy Abodes of Vishnu) – principal centres of worship of the deity in Vaishnavism. The temple, constructed in the Dravidian style of architecture, is glorified in the Divya Prabandha, the early medieval Tamil literature canon of the Tamil Alvar saints (6th-9th centuries CE), with structural additions to it made throughout the 16th century CE, when its ornate Gopuram was constructed. The Temple is a replica of the famous Sri Adikesavaperumal Temple at Thiruvattar. Sree Padmanabhaswamy Temple gave its name to Kerala's state capital Thiruvananthapuram. 'Thiru' 'Anantha' 'Puram' means Sacred Abode of Lord Anantha Padmanabha. The city is also known as Anandapuram (City of Bliss) and Syananduram (Where Bliss is not far off). Ananda refers to Sree Padmanabha Himself. Hindu scriptures refer to the Supreme Being as 'Sachidananda' (Absolute Truth, Absolute Consciousness and Absolute Bliss).

The principal deity, Padmanabhaswamy, is enshrined in the "Anantha-sayanam" posture (in the eternal sleep of Yoga-nidra on the serpent Anantha). The Maharajah of Travancore bears the title, "Sree Padmanabha-dasa' (Slave of Lord Padmanabha).

Origins of the Temple

There are many legends regarding the origins of the temple.

One such legend says that Vilvamangalathu Swamiyar alias Divakara Muni residing near Ananthapuram Temple, Kasargod prayed to Lord Vishnu for his darshan. The Lord came in disguise as a small, mischievous boy. The boy defiled the Saligrama which was kept for *puja*. The Sage became enraged at this and chased the boy. The boy disappeared. The Sage reached Ananthankadu searching for the boy. There he saw the boy merging into an Iluppa tree (Indian Butter Tree). The tree fell down and became Anantha Sayana Moorti (Vishnu reclining on Anantha). But the Lord was of an extraordinarily large size with head at Thiruvallom, navel at Thiruvananthapuram and lotus-feet at Thrippadapuram (Thrippappur). The Sage requested the Lord to shrink to a smaller proportion – thrice the length of his staff. Immediately, the Lord shrank. But even then many Iluppa trees obstructed a complete vision of the Lord. The Sage saw the Lord in three parts – thirumukham, thiruvudal and thrippadam.

Sree Padmanabhaswamy Temple

Ananthankadu Nagaraja Temple still exists to the north west of Sree Padmanabhaswamy Temple. The Samadhi (final resting place) of the Swamiyar exists to the west of the Sri Padmanabha Temple. A Krishna Temple was built over the Samadhi. This Temple, known as Vilvamangalam Sri Krishna Swami Temple, belongs to Thrissur Naduvil Madhom.

Main Shrine

In the sanctum sanctorum, Sree Padmanabha reclines on the serpent Anantha or Adi Sesha. The serpent has five hoods facing inwards, signifying contemplation. The Lord's right hand is placed over a Shiva lingam. Sridevi, the Goddess of Prosperity and Bhudevi, the Goddess of Earth, two consorts of Vishnu are by his side. Brahma emerges on a lotus, which emanates from the navel of the Lord. The idol is made from 12,000 saligramams. These saligrams are from the banks of the Gandaki River in Nepal, and to commemorate this certain rituals used to be performed at the Pashupatinath Temple. The idol of Sree Padmanabha is covered with, "Katusarkara yogam", a special ayurvedic mix, which forms a plaster that keeps the deity clean. The daily worship is with flowers and for the abhishekam, special deities are used.

The platforms in front of the vimanam and where the deity rests, are both carved out of a single massive stone and hence called "Ottakkal Mandapam." The Ottakkal Mandapam were cut out of a rock at Thirumala, about 4 miles north of the temple, measuring 20 feet square and 2.5 feet thick was brought and placed in front of the idol in the month of Edavom 906 M.E. (1731 CE). In order to perform *darshan* and *puja*, one has to ascend the to the mandapam. The deity is visible through three doors – the visage of the reclining Lord and Shiva lingam underneath the hand is seen through the first door; Sridevi and Divakara Muni in Katusarkara, Brahma seated on a lotus emanating from the Lord's navel, hence the name, "Padmanabha", gold *abhisheka moorthies* of Lord Padmanabha, Sridevi and Bhudevi, and silver *utsava moorthi* of Padmanabha through the second door; the Lord's feet, and Bhudevi and Kaundinya Muni in Katusarkara through the third door. Only the King of Travancore may perform *sashtanga namaskaram*, or prostrate on the "Ottakkal Mandapam". It is traditionally held that anybody who prostrates on the Mandapam has surrendered all that he possesses to the deity. Since the ruler has already done that, he is permitted to prostrate on this Mandapam.

Among the six *kallaras* or chambers in the Temple, Chamber B is very closely associated with Sree Padmanabhaswamy. It is not a part of the Temple Treasury. The holy Chamber houses a Srichakram, an idol of Sree Padmanabha and many valuables meant to enhance the potency of the principal deity. It also has in it the presence of many Gods and sages worshipping the Lord.

Inside the Temple, there are two other important shrines, Thekkedom and Thiruvambadi, for the deities, Sree Yoga Narasimha and Sree Krishna Swami respectively. One of the duties assigned to Lord Narasimha is protection of Chamber B. Thiruvambadi shrine enjoys an independent status and predates the shrine of Sree Padmanabha. Thiruvambadi shrine has its own Namaskara Mandapam, Bali stones and flagmast. The Lord of Thiruvambadi is Parthasarathi, the Divine Charioteer of Arjuna. The granite idol of the Lord of Thiruvambadi was brought from Gujarat by seventy-two families of Vrishni Vamsa Kshatriyas. As these Vrishnies belong to the lineage of Lord Krishna, they are known as Krishnan vakakkar. The two-armed granite idol, with one hand holding the whip and the other resting on the left thigh holding the conch close to it, is in standing posture. On Ekadasi days, the Lord is dressed and decorated as Mohini. There are also shrines for Sree Rama accompanied by Sita, Lakshmana and Hanuman, Vishwaksena (the Nirmalyadhari of Vishnu and Remover of Obstacles), Vyasa, Ganapati, Sasta and Kshetrapala (who guards the temple). Grand idols of Garuda and Hanuman stand with folded hands in the Valiya balikkal area.

Gopuram

The foundation of the present Gopuram was laid in 1566. The temple has a 100-foot, seven-tier Gopuram made in the Pandyan style. The temple stands by the side of a tank, named Padma Theertham (meaning the lotus spring). The temple has a corridor with 365 and one-quarter sculptured granite-stone pillars with elaborate carvings which stands out to be an ultimate testimonial for the Vishwakarma Sthapathis in sculpting this architectural masterpiece. This corridor extends from the eastern side into the sanctum sanctorum. An eighty-foot flag-staff stands in front of the main entry from the Prakaram(closed precincts of a temple). The ground floor under the Gopuram (main entrance in the eastern side) is known as the 'Nataka Sala' where the famous temple art Kathakali was staged in the night during the ten-day uthsavam (festival) conducted twice a year, during the Malayalam months of Meenam and Thulam.

Swamiyar, Tantri and Nambi

Temples where 'Swamiyar Pushpanjali' is conducted are claimants to extra sanctity. Sannyasins from any one of the monasteries founded by the disciples of Adi Sankara in Thrissur do *pushpanjali* (flower worship) daily to Sree Padmanabha, Narasimha Moorthi and Sri Krishna Swami. Of these monasteries, Naduvil Madhom is the most important as Vilvamangalathu Swamiyar, the founder of this Temple, belonged to this monastery.

The Nedumpalli Tharananallur Nambuthiripads of Iranjalakkuda have historically been the Tantries of the Temple. The Nambies, altogether four in number, are the Chief Priests of the Temple. Two Nambies – Periya Nambi and Panchagavyathu Nambi – are allotted to Sri Padmanabha and one Nambi each to Narasimha Moorthi and Sri Krishna Swami. The Nambies hail from either side of the Chandragiri River. They are anointed by the Pushpanjali Swamiyar.

History

The Kerala Mahatmyam (an Upa Purana deriving its origin from the Bhoogola Purana) is in the form of a discourse between Yudhishthira and the Sage Garga. It stated that Parashurama after founding Kerala divided the land into 64 gramas, crowned Bhanu Vicrama at Sreevardhanapuram (Padmanabhapuram), and styled him the Kovil Adhikarikal, i.e., the manager of the pagoda of Sreevalumcode (Thiruvananthapuram).

In earlier years, starting 225 M.E. (1050 C.E.) the Padmanabhaswamy Temple and its property were controlled by Thiruvananthapuram Sabha and later by Ettara Yogam with the assistance of Ettuveetil Pillamar. The Pushpanjali Swamiyars of Sree Padmanabhaswamy Temple preside over the meetings of Thiruvanandapuram Sabha and Ettara Yogam. In the past, the Swamiyars of Naduvil Madhom were appointed as Pushpanjali Swamiyars by the Crown Prince of Travancore, Thrippappoor Mootha Thiruvadi, with the concurrence of Ettara Yogam.

In the first half of the 18th century, in line with matrilineal customs, King Anizham Thirunal Marthanda Varma age 23, succeeded his uncle, King Rama Varma. He successfully suppressed the 700-year stranglehold of the Ettuveetil Pillais and his cousins following the discovery of conspiracies in which the lords were involved in against the Royal House of Travancore. The last major renovation of the Padmanabhaswamy temple commenced immediately after Anizham Thirunal's accession to the musnud and the idol was reconsecrated in 906 M.E. (1731 C.E.). On 17 January, 1750 C.E., Anizham Thirunal surrendered the kingdom of Travancore to Sree Padmanabha Swamy, the deity at the temple, and pledged that he and his descendants would be vassals or agents of the deity who would serve the kingdom as Padmanabha Dasa. Since then, the name of every Travancore king was preceded by the title Padmanabha Dasa; the female members of the royal family were called Padmanabha Sevinis. The donation of the kingdom to Sree Padmanabhaswamy was known as Thrippadi-danam. The final wishes of Anizham Thirunal on his passing at the age of 53 clearly delineated the historical relationship between the Maharajah and the temple: "That no deviation whatsoever should be made in regard to the dedication of the kingdom to Sree Padmanabhaswamy and that all future territorial acquisitions should be made over to the Devaswom."

Anizham Thirunal curtailed the authority of Ettara Yogam and it became an advisory and assenting body thereafter. Besides Naduvil Madhom, Munchira Madhom got the right to Pushpanjali during his reign. In the recent past, Uthradom Thirunal Marthanda Varma gave Pushpanjali rights to the Swamiyars of Thrikkaikattu Madhom and Thekke Madhom as well. Though the Maharajah is the appointing authority of the Pushpanjali Swamiyar, the former must do 'vechu namaskaram' when he sees the Swamiyar.

References to the Temple

The Divya Prabandha canon of Tamil literature by the Alvars glorifies this shrine as one of 13 Divya Desams in Malanadu. The 8th century Alvar Nammalvar sang the glories of Sree Padmanabha. But, the shrine is many centuries older as there are references to this temple in seven Puranas namely Bhagavata, Brahma, Brahmanda, Skanda, Varaha, Padma and Matsya. Syanandura Purana Samuchaya in Sanskrit and Ananta Pura Varnanam in Malayalam are two works that give detailed information of the temple city.

Temple Treasures and Assets

The temple and its assets belong to Lord Padmanabhaswamy, and are controlled by a trust run by the Royal family. The Kerala High Court ordered the temple and its assets be managed by the State on 31 January, 2011. As trustees of the temple, the Travancore Royal family have challenged the Kerala High Court's decision in the Supreme Court of India.

In June 2011, the Supreme Court directed the authorities from the archaeology department and fire services to open the secret chambers of the temple for inspection of the items kept inside.The temple has 6 vaults (*Kallaras*), labelled as A to F for book keeping purpose by the Court. While vaults A and B have been unopened over the past many years, vaults C to F have been opened from time to time. The two priests of the temple, the 'Periya Nambi' and the 'Thekkedathu Nambi', are the custodians of the four vaults, C to F, which are opened periodically. The Supreme Court had directed that "the existing practices, procedures and rituals" of the temple be followed while opening vaults C to F and using the articles inside. Vaults A and B shall be opened only for the purpose of making an inventory of the articles and then closed.

The review of the temple's underground vaults was undertaken by a seven-member panel appointed by the Supreme Court of India to generate an inventory, leading to the enumeration of a vast collection of articles that are traditionally kept under lock and key. A detailed inventory of the temple assets, consisting of gold, jewels, and other valuables was made. Several 18th century Napoleonic era coins were found, as well as a three-and-a-half feet tall gold idol of Mahavishnu studded with rubies and emeralds, and ceremonial attire for adorning the deity in the form of 16-part gold anki weighing almost 30 kilograms (66 lb) together with gold coconut shells, one studded with rubies and emeralds.

This revelation has solidified the status of the Padmanabhaswamy temple as one of the wealthiest temples in India and with the final estimate of the wealth, it might overtake the Tirumala Venkateswara Temple – hitherto thought to be the wealthiest temple – having some 320 billion (US$6.49 billion) in gold, coins and other assets. It is estimated that the value of the monumental items is close to 1.2 trillion (US$24.34 billion), making it the richest temple in the world. If the antique value is taken into account, these assets could be worth ten times the current market price.

The valuables are thought to have been in the temple for hundreds of years, having been put there by the Maharajahs of Travancore. While some Historians have suggested that a major chunk of the stored riches reached the kings in the form of tax, gifts, as well as conquered wealth of states and offerings stocked in the temple for safekeeping. But it has to be remembered that in Travancore a distinction was always made among Government Treasury (Karuvelam), Temple Treasury (Thiruvara Bhandaram or Sri Bhandaram) and the Royal Treasury (Chellam). During the reign of Maharani Gowri Lakshmi Bayi, hundreds of temples that were mismanaged were brought under the Government. The excess ornaments in these temples were transferred to the vaults of Sree Padmanabhaswamy Temple. Instead the funds of Sree Padmanabha Temple were utilised for the daily upkeep of these temples.

A ferry transported traders, pilgrims and chroniclers across the Gulf of Mannar from the Tenavaram temple, the famously wealthy Vishnu-Shiva temple town emporium to the Chera kingdom via Puttalam of the Jaffna kingdom during the medieval period. This temple was destroyed in 1587 CE, a few years after the Thiruvananthapuram Padmanabhaswamy temple gopuram was constructed. Morrocan traveller Ibn Batuta visited Tenavaram in the 14th century and described the Vishnu idol here as being made of gold and the size of a man with two large rubies as eyes “that lit up like lanterns during the night”. All people living within the vicinity of the temple and who visited it were fed with monetary endowments that were made to the idol.

On 4 July, 2011 the seven-member expert team tasked with taking stock of the temple assets decided to postpone opening of the chamber marked ‘B’. This chamber is sealed with an iron door with the image of a cobra on it and it has not been opened, due to the belief opening it would result in much misfortune. The royal family said that many legends were attached to the temple and that chamber B has a model of a snake on the main door and opening it could be a bad omen. An Ashtamangala Devaprasnam conducted in the Temple to discern the will of the Lord revealed that any attempts to open the Chamber B would cause Divine displeasure and that the holy articles in the other chambers were defiled in the inventorying process.

The Search for Lost Biblical Treasures

The Ark of the Covenant

The Ark of the Covenant (Hebrew: Aron Habrit), also known as the Ark of the Testimony, is a chest described in Book of Exodus as solely containing the Tablets of Stone on which the Ten Commandments were inscribed. According to some traditional interpretations of the Book of Exodus, Book of Numbers, and Epistle to the Hebrews, the Ark also contained Aaron's rod and a jar of manna. However, Books of Kings is categoric in declaring that the Ark contained only the two Tablets of the Law. According to the Book of Exodus, the Ark was built at the command of God, in accordance with the instructions given to Moses on Mount Sinai. God was said to have communicated with Moses "from between the two cherubim" on the Ark's cover. Rashi and some Midrashim suggest that there were two arks – a temporary one made by Moses himself, and a later one constructed by Bezalel.

The Ark of the Covenant

The Biblical account relates that during the Israelites' exodus from Egypt, the Ark was carried by the priests some 2,000 cubits in advance of the people and their army, or host. When the Ark was borne by priests into the bed of the Jordan, water in the river separated, opening a pathway for the entire host to pass through (Josh. 3:15-16; 4:7-18). The city of Jericho was taken with no more than a shout after the Ark of the Covenant was paraded for seven days around its wall by seven priests sounding seven trumpets of rams' horns (Josh. 6:4-20). When carried, the Ark was always wrapped in a veil, in tachash skins and a blue cloth, and was carefully concealed, even from the eyes of the Kohanim who carried it. There are no contemporary extra-Biblical references to the Ark.

Biblical Account

Construction and Description

According to the Book of Exodus, God instructed Moses on Mount Sinai during his 40-day stay upon the mountain within the thick cloud and darkness where God was (Ex. 19:20; 24:18) and he was shown the pattern for the tabernacle and furnishings of the Ark to be made of shittim-wood to house the Tablets of Stone. Moses instructed Bezalel and Oholiab to construct the Ark (Exodus 31).

The Book of Exodus gives detailed instructions on how the Ark is to be constructed. It is to be 2½ cubits in length, 1½ in breadth, and 1½ in height (as 21⁄2×11⁄2×11⁄2 royal cubits or 1.31×0.79×0.79 m). Then it is to be plated entirely with gold, and a crown or molding of gold is to be put around it. Four rings of gold are to be attached – two on each side – and through these rings staves of shittim-wood overlaid with gold for carrying the Ark are to be inserted; and these are not to be removed. A golden cover, adorned with golden cherubim, is to be placed above the Ark. The Ark is finally to be placed behind a veil (Parochet), a full description of which is also given.

Mobile Vanguard

After its creation by Moses, the Ark was carried by the Israelites during their 40-years of wandering in the desert. Whenever the Israelites camped, the Ark was placed in a special and sacred tent, the Tabernacle.

When the Israelites, led by Joshua toward the Promised Land, arrived at the banks of the River Jordan, the Ark was carried in the lead preceding the people and was the signal for their advance (Joshua 3:3, 6). During the crossing, the river grew dry as soon as the feet of the priests carrying the Ark touched its waters, and remained so until the priests – with the Ark – left the river after the people had passed over (Josh. 3:15-17; 4:10, 11, 18). As memorials, twelve stones were taken from the Jordan at the place where the priests had stood (Josh. 4:1-9).

In the Battle of Jericho, the Ark was carried round the city once a day for seven days, preceded by the armed men and seven priests sounding seven trumpets of rams' horns (Josh. 6:4-15). On the seventh day, the seven priests sounding the seven trumpets of rams' horns before the Ark compassed the city seven times and, with a great shout, Jericho's wall fell down flat and the people took the city (Josh. 6:16-20). After the defeat at Ai, Joshua lamented before the Ark (Josh. 7:6-9). When Joshua read the Law to the people between Mount Gerizim and Mount Ebal, they stood on each side of the Ark. The Ark was again set up by Joshua at Shiloh, but when the Israelites fought against Benjamin at Gibeah, they had the Ark with them and consulted it after their defeat.

Capture by the Philistines

The Ark is next spoken of as being in the Tabernacle at Shiloh during Samuel's apprenticeship (1 Sam. 3:3). After the settlement of the Israelites in Canaan, the Ark remained in the Tabernacle at Gilgal for a season before being removed to Shiloh until the time of Eli, between 300 and 400 years (Jeremiah 7:12), when it was carried into the field of battle, so as to secure, as they had hoped, victory to the Hebrews. The Ark was taken by the Philistines (1 Sam. 4:3-11) who subsequently sent it back after retaining it for seven months (1 Sam. 5:7, 8) because of the events said to have transpired.

After their first defeat at Eben-ezer, the Israelites had the Ark brought from Shiloh, and welcomed its coming with great rejoicing. In the second battle, the Israelites were again defeated, and the Philistines captured the Ark (1 Sam. 4:3-5, 10, 11). The news of its capture was at once taken to Shiloh by a messenger "with his clothes rent, and with earth upon his head". The old priest, Eli, fell dead when he heard it; and his daughter-in-law, bearing a son at the time the news of the capture of the Ark was received, named him Ichabod – explained as "Where is glory?" in reference to the loss of the Ark (1 Sam. 4:12-22).

The Philistines took the Ark to several places in their country, and at each place misfortune befell them (1 Sam. 5:1-6). At Ashdod it was placed in the temple of Dagon. The next morning Dagon was found prostrate, bowed down, before it; and on being restored to his place, he was on the following morning again found prostrate and broken. The people of Ashdod were smitten with tumors; a plague of rats was sent over the land (1 Sam. 6:5). The affliction of boils was also visited upon the people of Gath and of Ekron, whither the Ark was successively removed (1 Sam. 5:8-12).

After the Ark had been among them for seven months, the Philistines, on the advice of their diviners, returned it to the Israelites, accompanying its return with an offering consisting of golden images of the tumors and rats wherewith they had been afflicted. The Ark was set in the field of Joshua the Bethshemite, and the Bethshemites offered sacrifices and burnt offerings (1 Sam. 6:1-15). Out of curiosity, the men of Beth-shemesh gazed at the Ark; and as a punishment, seventy of them (fifty thousand seventy in some ms.) were smitten by the Lord (1 Sam. 6:19). The Bethshemites sent to Kirjath-jearim, or Baal-Judah, to have the Ark removed (1 Sam. 6:21); and it was taken to the house of Abinadab, whose son Eleazar was sanctified to keep it. Kirjath-jearim remained the abode of the Ark for twenty years. Under Saul, the Ark was with the army before he first met the Philistines, but the king was too impatient to consult it before engaging in battle. In 1 Chronicle, 13:3, it is stated that the people were not accustomed to consult the Ark in the days of Saul.

In the Days of King David

At the beginning of his reign, King David removed the Ark from Kirjath-jearim amid great rejoicing. On the way to Zion, Uzzah, one of the drivers of the cart whereon the Ark was carried, put out his hand to steady the Ark, and was smitten by God for touching it. David, in fear, carried the Ark aside into the house of Obed-edom the Gittite, instead of carrying it on to Zion, and there it stayed three months (2 Samuel 6:1-11; 1 Chronicles 13:1-13).

On hearing that God had blessed Obed-edom because of the presence of the Ark in his house, David had the Ark brought to Zion by the Levites, while he himself, girded with a linen ephod, danced before the Lord with all his might and in the sight of all the public gathered in Jerusalem – a performance that caused him to be scornfully rebuked by his first wife, Saul's daughter Michal (2 Sam. 6:12-16, 20-22; 1 Chron.

15). In Zion, David put the Ark in the tabernacle he had prepared for it, offered sacrifices, distributed food, and blessed the people and his own household (2 Sam. 6:17-20; 1 Chron. 16:1-3; 2 Chron. 1:4).

The Levites were appointed to minister before the Ark (1 Chron. 16:4). David's plan of building a temple for the Ark was stopped at the advice of God (2 Sam. 7:1-17; 1 Chron. 17:1-15; 28:2, 3). The Ark was with the army during the siege of Rabbah (2 Sam. 11:11); and when David fled from Jerusalem at the time of Absalom's conspiracy, the Ark was carried along with him until he ordered Zadok the priest to return it to Jerusalem (2 Sam. 15:24-29).

In Solomon's Temple

When Abiathar was dismissed from the priesthood by King Solomon for having taken part in Adonijah's conspiracy against David, his life was spared because he had formerly borne the Ark (1 Kings 2:26). Solomon worshipped before the Ark after his dream in which God promised him wisdom (1 Kings 3:15).

During the construction of Solomon's Temple, a special inner room, named Kodesh Hakodashim (Eng. Holy of Holies), was prepared to receive and house the Ark (1 Kings 6:19); and when the Temple was dedicated, the Ark – containing the original tablets of the Ten Commandments – was placed therein (1 Kings 8:6-9). When the priests emerged from the holy place after placing the Ark there, the Temple was filled with a cloud, "for the glory of the Lord had filled the house of the Lord" (1 Kings 8:10-11; 2 Chron. 5:13, 14).

When Solomon married Pharaoh's daughter, he caused her to dwell in a house outside Zion, as Zion was consecrated because of its containing the Ark (2 Chron. 8:11). King Josiah had the Ark put in the Temple (2 Chron. 35:3), whence it appears to have again been removed by one of his successors.

The Babylonian Conquest and aftermath

In 586 BC, the Babylonians destroyed Jerusalem and Solomon's Temple. There is no record of what became of the Ark.

Book of Revelation

According to the Christian New Testament Book of Revelation, the Ark is in the Temple of God in Heaven in vision: "Then God's temple in heaven was opened, and within his temple was seen the Ark of his Covenant" (Rev. 11:19 NIV).

References to the Ark in Scripture

Jewish Tanakh

The Ark is first mentioned in the Book of Exodus, and then numerous times in Deuteronomy, Joshua, Judges, I Samuel, II Samuel, I Kings, I Chronicles, II Chronicles, Psalms and Jeremiah. In the Book of Jeremiah, it is referenced by Jeremiah, who, speaking in the days of Josiah (Jer. 3:16), prophesied a future time when the Ark will no longer be talked about or be made again.

Second Book of Maccabees

In the Jewish Deuterocanonical book Second Maccabees, Chapter 2, "one finds in the records" that Jeremiah, having received an oracle of the Lord, ordered that the tent and the Ark and the altar of incense should follow him to the mountain of God where he sealed them up in a cave, and he told those who followed him in order to mark the way, but they could not find it. "The place shall remain unknown until God gathers his people together again and shows his mercy, and then the Lord will disclose these things, and the glory of the Lord and the cloud shall appear, as they were shown in the case of Moses, and as Solomon asked that the place be specially consecrated." 2 Maccabees 2:4-8

Christian New Testament

In the New Testament, the Ark is mentioned in the Epistle to the Hebrews and the Revelation to St. John. Hebrews 9:4 states that the Ark contained "the golden pot that had manna, and Aaron's rod that budded, and the tablets of the covenant". Revelation 11:19 says the prophet saw God's temple in heaven opened, "and the ark of his covenant was seen within his temple".

A number of Roman Catholic writers connect this verse with the Woman of the Apocalypse in Revelation 12:1, which immediately follows, and argue that the Blessed Virgin Mary is the "Ark of the New Covenant." Carrying the saviour of mankind within her, she herself became the Holy of Holies. This is the interpretation given in the fourth century by Saint Ambrose, Saint Ephraem of Syria and Saint Augustine. Athanasius the bishop of Alexandria wrote about the connections between the Ark and the Virgin Mary: "O noble Virgin, truly you are greater than any other greatness. For who is your equal in greatness, O dwelling place of God the Word? To whom among all creatures shall I compare you, O Virgin? You are greater than them all O (Ark of the) Covenant, clothed with purity instead of gold! You are the Ark in which is found the golden vessel containing the true manna, that is, the flesh in which Divinity resides" (Homily of the Papyrus of Turin).

Qur'an

In chapter 2 of the Islamic Qur'an (Verse 248), the Children of Israel, at the time of Samuel and Saul, were given back the Tabut E Sakina (the casket of Shekhinah) which contained remnants of the household of Musa (Moses) and Harun (Aaron) carried by angels which confirmed peace and reassurance for them from their Lord. The Qur'an states:

And (further) their Prophet said to them: "A Sign of His authority is that there shall come to you the Ark of the covenant, with (an assurance) therein of security (Sakina) from your Lord, and the relics left by the family of Moses and the family of Aaron, carried by angels. In this is a symbol for you if ye indeed have faith.

The Islamic scholar Al Baidawi mentioned that the sakina could be Tawrat, the Books of Moses. According to Al-Jalalan, the relics in the Ark were the fragments of the two tablets, rods, robes, shoes, mitres of Moses and the vase of manna. Al-Tha'alibi, in Qisas Al-Anbiya (The Stories of the Prophets), has given an earlier and later history of the Ark.

According to most Muslim scholars, the Ark of the Covenant has a religious basis in Islam, and Islam gives it special significance. Shia sect of Muslims believe that it will be found by Mahdi near the end of times from Lake Tiberias.

Rumoured Current Locations

Since its disappearance from the Biblical narrative, there have been a number of claims of having discovered or having possession of the Ark, and several possible places have been suggested for its location.

Mount Nebo

Maccabees 2:4-10, written around 100 BC, says that the prophet Jeremiah, "being warned by God" before the Babylonian invasion, took the Ark, the Tabernacle, and the Altar of Incense, and buried them in a cave on Mount Nebo (Jordan), informing those of his followers who wished to find the place that it should remain unknown "until the time that God should gather His people again together, and receive them unto mercy."

Ethiopia

The Ethiopian Orthodox Church claims to possess the Ark of the Covenant, or Tabot, in Axum. The object is currently kept under guard in a treasury near the Church of Our Lady Mary of Zion and is used occasionally in ritual processions. Replicas of the Axum tabot are kept in every Ethiopian church, each with its own dedication to a particular saint, the most popular of these include Mary, George and Michael.

The Kebra Nagast, composed to legitimise the new dynasty ruling Ethiopia following its establishment in 1270, narrates how the real Ark of the Covenant was brought to Ethiopia by Menelik I with divine assistance, while a forgery was left in the Temple in Jerusalem. Although the Kebra Nagast is the best-known account of this belief, the belief predates the document. Abu Salih, the Armenian, writing in the last quarter of the twelfth century, makes one early reference to this belief that they possessed the Ark. "The Abyssinians possess also the Ark of the Covenant", he wrote, and, after a description of the object, describes how the liturgy is celebrated upon the Ark four times a year, "on the feast of the great nativity, on the feast of the glorious Baptism, on the feast of the holy Resurrection, and on the feast of the illuminating Cross."

On 25 June, 2009, the patriarch of the Orthodox Church of Ethiopia, Abune Paulos, said he would announce to the world the next day the unveiling of the Ark of the Covenant, which he said had been kept safe and secure in a church in Axum, Ethiopia. The following day, on 26 June, 2009, the patriarch announced that he would not unveil the Ark after all, but that instead he could attest to its current status.

Southern Africa

The Lemba people of South Africa and Zimbabwe have claimed that their ancestors carried the Ark south, calling it the ngoma lungundu or "voice of God", eventually hiding it in a deep cave in the Dumghe mountains, their spiritual home.

On 14 April, 2008, in a UK Channel 4 documentary broadcast, Tudor Parfitt, taking a literalist approach to the Biblical story, described his research into this claim. He says that the object described by the Lemba has attributes similar to the Ark. It was of similar size, was carried on poles by priests, was not allowed to touch the ground, was revered as a voice of their God, and was used as a weapon of great power, sweeping enemies aside.

In his book, *The Lost Ark of the Covenant* (2008), Parfitt also suggests that the Ark was taken to Arabia following the Second Book of Maccabees, and cites Arabic sources which maintain it was brought in distant times to Yemen. One Lemba clan, the Buba, which was supposed to have brought the Ark to Africa, have a genetic signature called the Cohen Modal Haplotype. This suggests a male Semitic link to the Levant. Lemba tradition maintains that the Ark spent some time in Sena in Yemen. Later, it was taken across the sea to East Africa and may have been taken inland at the time of the Great Zimbabwe civilisation. According to their oral traditions, sometime after the arrival of the Lemba with the Ark, it self-destructed. Using a core from the original, the Lemba priests constructed a new one. This replica was discovered in a cave by a Swedish German missionary named Harald von Sicard in the 1940s and eventually found its way to the Museum of Human Science in Harare.

Parfitt had this artefact radio-carbon – dated to about 1350 AD, which coincided with the sudden end of the Great Zimbabwe civilisation.

Europe

Chartres Cathedral, France

French author Louis Charpentier claimed that the Ark was taken to Chartres Cathedral by the Knights Templar.

Rennes-le-Château, Then to America

Several recent authors have theorised that the Ark was taken from Jerusalem to the village of Rennes-le-Château in Southern France. Karen Ralls has cited Freemason Patrick Byrne, who believes the Ark was moved from Rennes-le-Château at the outbreak of World War I to America.

Italy

The Ark of the Covenant is alleged to be kept in the Basilica of St. John Lateran, surviving the pillages of Rome by Genseric and Alaric I.

United Kingdom

In 2003, author Graham Phillips hypothetically concluded that the Ark was taken to Mount Sinai in the Valley of Edom by the Maccabees. Phillips claims it remained there until the 1180s, when Ralph de Sudeley, the leader of the Templars found the Maccabean treasure at Jebel al-Madhbah, returned home to his estate at Herdewyke in Warwickshire, UK, taking the treasure with him.

Ireland

During the turn of the 20th century, British Israelites carried out some excavations of the Hill of Tara in Ireland looking for the Ark of the Covenant – the Royal Society of Antiquaries of Ireland campaigned successfully to have them stopped before they destroyed the hill.

The Search for the Holy Grail

The Holy Grail is a mythical sacred object figuring in literature and certain Christian traditions, most often identified with the dish, plate, or cup used by Jesus at the Last Supper and said to possess miraculous powers. The connection of Joseph of Arimathea with the Grail legend dates from Robert de Boron's Joseph d'Arimathie (late 12th century) in which Joseph receives the Grail from an apparition of Jesus and sends it with his followers to Great Britain; building upon this theme, later writers recounted how Joseph used the Grail to catch Christ's blood while interring him and that in Britain he founded a line of guardians to keep it safe. The quest for the Holy Grail makes up an important segment of the Arthurian cycle, appearing first in works by Chrétien de Troyes. The legend may combine Christian lore with a Celtic myth of a cauldron endowed with special powers.

The Holy Grail

The Grail legend's development has been traced in detail by cultural historians: It is a legend which first came together in the form of written romances, deriving perhaps from some pre-Christian folklore hints, in the later 12th and early 13th centuries. The early Grail romances centred on Percival and were woven into the more general Arthurian fabric. Some of the Grail legend is interwoven with legends of the Holy Chalice.

Origins

Grail

The Grail plays a different role everywhere it appears, but in most versions of the legend, the hero must prove himself worthy to be in its presence. In the early tales, Percival's immaturity prevents him from fulfilling his destiny when he first encounters the Grail, and he must grow spiritually and mentally before he can locate it again. In later tellings, the Grail is a symbol of God's grace, available to all but only fully realised by those who prepare themselves spiritually, like the saintly Galahad.

Early Forms

There are two veins of thought concerning the Grail's origin. The first, championed by Roger Sherman Loomis, Alfred Nutt, and Jessie Weston, holds that it derived from early Celtic myth and folklore. Loomis traced a number of parallels between Medieval Welsh literature and Irish material and the Grail romances, including similarities between the Mabinogion's Bran the Blessed and the Arthurian Fisher King, and between Bran's life-restoring cauldron and the Grail. On the other hand, some scholars believe the Grail began as a purely Christian symbol. For example, Joseph Goering of the University of Toronto has identified sources for Grail imagery in 12th century wall paintings from churches in the Catalan Pyrenees (now mostly removed to the Museu Nacional d'Art de Catalunya, Barcelona), which present unique iconic images of the Virgin Mary holding a bowl that radiates tongues of fire, images that predate the first literary account by Chrétien de Troyes. Goering argues that they were the original inspiration for the Grail legend.

Another recent theory holds that the earliest stories that cast the Grail in a Christian light were meant to promote the Roman Catholic sacrament of the Holy Communion. Although the practice of Holy Communion was first alluded to in the Christian Bible and defined by theologians in the 1st centuries AD, it was around the time of the appearance of the first Christianized Grail literature that the Roman church was beginning to add more ceremony and mysticism around this particular sacrament. Thus, the first Grail stories may have been celebrations of a renewal in this traditional sacrament. This theory has some basis in the fact that the Grail legends are a phenomenon of the Western church.

In several articles, Daniel Scavone, professor Emeritus of history at the University of Southern Indiana, puts forward a hypothesis which identifies the Shroud of Turin as the real object that inspires the romances of the Holy Grail.

Most scholars today accept that both Christian and Celtic traditions contributed to the legend's development, though many of the early Celtic-based arguments are largely discredited (Loomis himself came to reject much of Weston and Nutt's work). The general view is that the central theme of the Grail is Christian, even when not explicitly religious, but that much of the setting and imagery of the early romances is drawn from Celtic material.

Etymology

The word graal, as it is earliest spelled, comes from Old French graal or greal, cognate with Old Provençal grazal and Old Catalan gresal, meaning "a cup or bowl of earth, wood, or metal" (or other various types of vessels in Southern French dialects). The most commonly accepted etymology derives it from Latin gradalis or gradale via an earlier form, cratalis, a derivative of crater or cratus which was, in turn, borrowed from Greek krater (a two-handed shallow cup). Alternate suggestions include a derivative of cratis, a name for a type of woven basket that came to refer to a dish, or a derivative of Latin gradus meaning "'by degree', 'by stages', applied to a dish brought to the table in different stages or services during a meal."

According to the Catholic Encyclopaedia, after the cycle of Grail romances was well established, late medieval writers came up with a false etymology for sangréal, an alternative name for "Holy Grail". In Old French, san graal or san gréal means "Holy Grail" and sang réal means "royal blood"; later writers played on this pun. Since then, "Sang real" is sometimes employed to lend a medievalizing air in referring to the Holy Grail. This connection with royal blood bore fruit in a modern bestseller linking many historical conspiracy theories.

Beginnings in Literature

Chrétien de Troyes

The Grail is first featured in Perceval, le Conte du Graal (The Story of the Grail) by Chrétien de Troyes, who claims he was working from a source book given to him by his patron, Count Philip of Flanders. In this incomplete poem, dated sometime between 1180 and 1191, the object has not yet acquired the implications of holiness it would have in later works. While dining in the magical abode of the Fisher King, Perceval witnesses a wondrous procession in which youths carry magnificent objects from one chamber to another, passing before him at each course of the meal. First comes a young man carrying a bleeding lance, then two boys carrying candelabras. Finally, a beautiful young girl emerges bearing an elaborately decorated graal, or Grail.

Chrétien refers to his object not as "The Grail" but as un graal, showing the word was used, in its earliest literary context, as a common noun. For Chrétien, the Grail was a wide, somewhat deep dish or bowl, interesting because it contained not a pike, salmon or lamprey, as the audience may have expected for such a container, but a single Mass wafer which provided sustenance for the Fisher King's crippled father. Perceval, who had been warned against talking too much, remains silent through all of this, and wakes up the next morning alone. He later learns that if he had asked the appropriate questions about what he saw, he would have healed his maimed host, much to his honour. The story of the Wounded King's mystical fasting is not unique; several saints were said to have lived without food besides communion, for instance Saint Catherine of Genoa. This may imply that Chrétien intended the Mass wafer to be the significant part of the ritual, and the Grail to be a mere prop.

Robert de Boron

Though Chrétien's account is the earliest and most influential of all Grail texts, it was in the work of Robert de Boron that the Grail truly became the "Holy Grail" and assumed the form most familiar to modern readers. In his verse, romance Joseph d'Arimathie, composed between 1191 and 1202, Robert tells the story of Joseph of Arimathea acquiring the chalice of the Last Supper to collect Christ's blood upon his removal from the cross. Joseph is thrown in prison, where Christ visits him and explains the mysteries of the blessed cup. Upon his release, Joseph gathers his in-laws and other followers and travels to the west, and founds a dynasty of Grail keepers that eventually includes Perceval.

Other Early Literature

After this point, Grail literature divides into two classes. The first concerns King Arthur's knights visiting the Grail castle or questing after the object; the second concerns the Grail's history in the time of Joseph of Arimathea.

The nine most important works from the first group are:

- The Perceval of Chrétien de Troyes.
- Four continuations of Chrétien's poem, by authors of differing vision and talent, designed to bring the story to a close.
- The German Parzival by Wolfram von Eschenbach, which adapted at least the holiness of Robert's Grail into the framework of Chrétien's story.
- The Didot Perceval, named after the manuscript's former owner, and purportedly a prosification of Robert de Boron's sequel to Joseph d'Arimathie.
- The Welsh romance Peredur, generally included in the Mabinogion, likely at least indirectly founded on Chrétien's poem but including very striking differences from it, preserving as it does elements of pre-Christian traditions such as the Celtic cult of the head.
- Perlesvaus, called the "least canonical" Grail romance because of its very different character.
- The German Diu Crône (The Crown), in which Gawain, rather than Perceval, achieves the Grail.
- The Lancelot section of the vast Vulgate Cycle, which introduces the new Grail hero, Galahad.
- The Queste del Saint Graal, another part of the Vulgate Cycle, concerning the adventures of Galahad and his achievement of the Grail.

Of the second class there are:

- Robert de Boron's Joseph d'Arimathie,
- The Estoire del Saint Graal, the first part of the Vulgate Cycle (but written after Lancelot and the Queste), based on Robert's tale but expanding it greatly with many new details.
- Verses by Rigaut de Barbezieux, a late 12 or early 13th century Provençal troubador, where mention is made of Perceval, the lance, and the Grail ("Like Perceval when he lived, who stood amazed in contemplation, so that he was quite unable to ask what purpose the lance and grail served" – "Attressi con Persavaus el temps que vivia,

que s'esbait d'esgarder tant qu'anc non saup demandar de que servia la lansa ni-l grazaus").

Though all these works have their roots in Chrétien, several contain pieces of tradition not found in Chrétien which are possibly derived from earlier sources.

Conceptions of the Grail

The Grail was considered a bowl or dish when first described by Chrétien de Troyes. Hélinand of Froidmont described a Grail as a "wide and deep saucer" (scutella lata et aliquantulum profunda). Other authors had their own ideas: Robert de Boron portrayed it as the vessel of the Last Supper; and Peredur had no Grail per se, presenting the hero instead with a platter containing his kinsman's bloody, severed head. In Parzival, Wolfram von Eschenbach, citing the authority of a certain (probably fictional) Kyot the Provençal, claimed the Grail was a stone that fell from Heaven (called lapsit exillis), and had been the sanctuary of the Neutral Angels who took neither side during Lucifer's rebellion. The authors of the Vulgate Cycle used the Grail as a symbol of divine grace. Galahad, illegitimate son of Lancelot and Elaine, the world's greatest knight and the Grail Bearer at the castle of Corbenic, is destined to achieve the Grail, his spiritual purity making him a greater warrior than even his illustrious father. Galahad and the interpretation of the Grail involving him were picked up in the 15th century by Sir Thomas Malory in Le Morte d'Arthur, and remain popular today.

Later Legend

Belief in the Grail and interest in its potential whereabouts has never ceased. Ownership has been attributed to various groups (including the Knights Templar, probably because they were at the peak of their influence around the time that Grail stories started circulating in the 12th and 13th centuries).

There are cups claimed to be the Grail in several churches, for instance the Saint Mary of Valencia Cathedral, which contains an artefact, the Holy Chalice, supposedly taken by Saint Peter to Rome in the 1st century, and then to Huesca in Spain by Saint Lawrence in the 3rd century. According to legend, the monastery of San Juan de la Peña, located at the south-west of Jaca, in the province of Huesca, Spain, protected the chalice of the Last Supper from the Islamic invaders of the Iberian Peninsula. Archaeologists say the artefact is a 1st century Middle Eastern stone vessel, possibly from Antioch, Syria (now Turkey); its history can be traced to the 11th century, and it now rests atop an ornate stem and base, made in the Medieval era of alabaster, gold, and gemstones. It was the official papal chalice for many Popes, and has been used by many others, most recently by Pope Benedict XVI, on July 9, 2006. The emerald chalice at Genoa, which was obtained during the Crusades at Caesarea Maritima at great cost, has been less championed as the Holy Grail since an accident on the road, while it was being returned from Paris after the fall of Napoleon, revealed that the emerald was green glass.

In Wolfram von Eschenbach's telling, the Grail was kept safe at the castle of Munsalvaesche (mons salvationis), entrusted to Titurel, the first Grail King. Some, not least the monks of Montserrat, have identified the castle with the real sanctuary of Montserrat in Catalonia, Spain. Other stories claim that the Grail is buried beneath Rosslyn Chapel or lies deep in the spring at Glastonbury Tor. Still other stories claim that a secret line of hereditary protectors keep the Grail, or that it was hidden by the Templars in Oak Island, Nova Scotia's famous "Money Pit", while local folklore in Accokeek, Maryland says that it was brought to the town by a closeted priest aboard Captain John Smith's ship. Turn of the century accounts state that Irish partisans of the Clan Dhuir (O'Dwyer, Dwyer) transported the Grail to the United States during the 19th century and the Grail was kept by their descendents in secrecy in a small abbey in the upper-Northwest (now believed to be Southern Minnesota).

Modern Interpretations

The story of the Grail and of the quest to find it became increasingly popular in the 19th century, referred to in literature such as Alfred Tennyson's Arthurian cycle the Idylls of the King. The combination of hushed reverence, chromatic harmonies and sexualised imagery in Richard Wagner's late opera Parsifal gave new significance to the grail theme, for the first time associating the grail – now periodically producing blood – directly with female fertility. The high seriousness of the subject was also epitomised in Dante Gabriel Rossetti's painting, in which a woman modelled by Jane Morris holds the Grail with one hand, while adopting a gesture of blessing with the other. Other artists, including George Frederic Watts and William Dyce also portrayed Grail subjects.

The Grail later turned up in movies; it debuted in a silent Parsifal. In *The Light of Faith* (1922), Lon Chaney attempted to steal it. *The Silver Chalice*, a novel about the Grail by Thomas B. Costain was made into a 1954 movie. *Lancelot du Lac* (1974) was made by Robert Bresson. *Monty Python and the Holy Grail* (1975) (adapted in 2004 as the stage production Spamalot) was a comedic adaptation. Excalibur attempted to restore a more traditional heroic representation of an Arthurian tale, in which the Grail is revealed as a mystical means to revitalise Arthur himself, and of the barren land to which his depressive sickness is connected. *Indiana Jones and the Last Crusade* and *The Fisher King* are more recent adoptions.

The Grail has been used as a theme in fantasy, historical fiction and science fiction; a quest for the Grail appears in Bernard Cornwell's series of books *The Grail Quest*, set during The Hundred Years War. Michael Moorcock's fantasy novel *The War Hound and the World's Pain* depicts a supernatural Grail quest set in the era of the Thirty Years' War, and science fiction has taken the Quest into interstellar space, figuratively in Samuel R. Delany's 1968 novel *Nova*, and literally on the television shows Babylon 5 and Stargate SG-1 (as the "Sangraal"). Marion Zimmer Bradley's *The Mists of Avalon* has the Grail as one of four objects symbolising the four elements: the Grail itself (water), the sword Excalibur (fire), a dish (earth), and a spear or wand (air). The Grail features heavily in the novels of Peter David's *Knight trilogy*, which depict King Arthur reappearing in modern-day New York City, in particular the second and third novels, *One Knight Only* and *Fall of Knight*. The Grail is central in many modern Arthurian works, including Charles Williams's novel *War in Heaven* and his two collections of poems about Taliessin, *Taliessin Through Logres* and *Region of the Summer Stars*, and in feminist author Rosalind Miles' *Child of the Holy Grail*. The Grail also features heavily in Umberto Eco's 2000 novel *Baudolino*.

The Grail has also been treated in works of non-fiction, which generally seek to interpret its meaning in novel ways. Such a tack was taken by psychologists Emma Jung and Marie-Louise von Franz, who utilised analytical psychology to interpret the Grail as a series of symbols in their book *The Grail Legend.* This type of interpretation had previously been utilised, in less detail, by Carl Jung, and was later invoked by Joseph Campbell.

Other works attempt to connect the Grail to conspiracy theories and esoteric traditions. In *The Sign and the Seal*, Graham Hancock asserts that the Grail story is a coded description of the stone tablets stored in the Ark of the Covenant. For the authors of *Holy Blood, Holy Grail*, who assert that their research ultimately reveals that Jesus may not have died on the cross, but lived to wed Mary Magdalene and father children whose Merovingian lineage continues today, the Grail is a mere sideshow: they say it is a reference to Mary Magdalene as the receptacle of Jesus' bloodline.

Such works have been the inspiration for a number of popular modern fiction novels. The best known is Dan Brown's bestselling novel *The Da Vinci Code*, which, like *Holy Blood, Holy Grail*, is based on the idea that the real Grail is not a cup but the womb and later the earthly remains of Mary Magdalene (again cast as Jesus' wife), plus a set of ancient documents claimed to tell the true story of Jesus, his teachings and descendants. In Brown's novel, it is hinted that Jesus was merely a mortal man with strong ideals, and that the Grail was long buried beneath Rosslyn Chapel in Scotland, but that in recent decades its guardians had it relocated to a secret chamber embedded in the floor beneath the Inverted Pyramid near the Louvre Museum. The latter location, like Rosslyn Chapel, has never been mentioned in real Grail lore.

The Spear of Destiny

The Holy Lance (also known as the Spear of Destiny, Holy Spear, Lance of Longinus, Spear of Longinus or Spear of Christ) is the name given to the lance that pierced Jesus' side as he hung on the cross in John's account of the Crucifixion.

Biblical References

The lance (Greek: longche) is mentioned only in the Gospel of John (19:31–37) and not in any of the Synoptic Gospels. The gospel states that the Romans planned to break Jesus' legs, a practice known as crucifragium, which was a method of hastening death during a crucifixion. Just before they did so, they realised that Jesus was already dead and that there was no reason to break his legs. To make sure that he was dead, a Roman soldier (named in extra-Biblical tradition as Longinus) stabbed him in the side.

A Roman soldier stabbed him in the side with a lance

... but one of the soldiers pierced his side with a lance, and immediately there came out blood and water.

– John 19:34

The phenomenon of blood and water was considered a miracle by Origen. Catholics generally choose to employ a more allegorical interpretation: it represents one of the main key teachings/mysteries of the Church, and one of the main themes of the Gospel of Matthew, which is the homoousian interpretation adopted by the First Council of Nicaea, that "Jesus Christ was both true God and true man". The blood symbolises his true humanity, the water his divinity. A ceremonial

Spear of Destiny
– Heilige Lance

remembrance of this is done when a Catholic priest says Mass. The priest pours a small amount of holy water into the wine before the consecration, an act which acknowledges Christ's humanity and divinity and recalls the issuance of blood and water from Christ's side on the cross.

Longinus

The name of the soldier who pierced Christ's side with a longche is not given in the Gospel of John, but in the oldest known references to the legend, the apocryphal Gospel of Nicodemus appended to late manuscripts of the 4th century Acts of Pilate, the soldier is identified as a centurion and called Longinus (making the spear's "correct" Latin name Lancea Longini).

A form of the name Longinus occurs on a miniature in the Rabula Gospels (conserved in the Laurentian Library, Florence), which was illuminated by one Rabulas in the year 586. In the miniature, the name LOGINOS is written in Greek characters above the head of the soldier who is thrusting his lance into Christ's side. This is one of the earliest records of the name, if the inscription is not a later addition.

Relics claimed to be the Holy Lance

There have been three or four major relics that are claimed to be the Holy Lance or parts of it.

Vatican Lance

No actual lance is known until the pilgrim Antoninus of Piacenza (AD 570), describing the holy places of Jerusalem, says that he saw in the Basilica of Mount Zion "the crown of thorns with which Our Lord was crowned and the lance with which He was struck in the side". A mention of the lance occurs in the so-called Breviarius at the Church of the Holy Sepulchre. The presence in Jerusalem of the relic is attested by Cassiodorus (c. 485 – c. 585) as well as by Gregory of Tours (c. 538 – 594), who had not actually been to Jerusalem.

In 615, Jerusalem and its relics were captured by the Persian forces of King Khosrau II (Chosroes II). According to the Chronicon Paschale, the point of the lance, which had been broken off, was given in the same year to Nicetas, who took it to Constantinople and deposited it in the church of Hagia Sophia, and later to the Church of the Virgin of the Pharos. This point of the lance, which was now set in an icon, was acquired by the Latin Emperor, Baldwin II of Constantinople, who later sold it to Louis IX of France. The point of the lance was then enshrined with the Crown of Thorns in the Sainte Chapelle in Paris. During the French Revolution these relics were removed to the Bibliothèque Nationale but subsequently disappeared. (The present "Crown of Thorns" is a wreath of rushes.)

As for the larger portion of the lance, Arculpus claimed he saw it at the Church of the Holy Sepulchre around 670 in Jerusalem, but there is otherwise no mention of it after the sack in 615. Some claim that the larger relic had been conveyed to Constantinople in the 8th century, possibly at the same time as the Crown of Thorns. At any rate, its presence at Constantinople seems to be clearly attested by various pilgrims, particularly Russians, and, though it was deposited in various churches in succession, it seems possible to trace it and distinguish it from the relic of the point. Sir John Mandeville declared in 1357 that he had seen the blade of the Holy Lance both at Paris and at Constantinople, and that the latter was a much larger relic than the former; it is worth adding that Mandeville is not generally regarded as one of the Middle Ages' most reliable witnesses, and his supposed travels are usually treated as an eclectic amalgam of myths, legends and other fictions. "The lance which pierced Our Lord's side" was among the relics at Constantinople shown in the 1430s to Pedro Tafur, who added, "God grant that in the overthrow of the Greeks they have not fallen into the hands of the enemies of the Faith, for they will have been ill-treated and handled with little reverence."

Whatever the Constantinople relic was, it did fall into the hands of the Turks, and in 1492, under circumstances minutely described in Pastor's History of the Popes, the Sultan Bayazid II sent it to Innocent VIII to encourage the pope to continue to keep his brother and rival Zizim (Cem) prisoner. At this time, great doubts as to its authenticity were felt at Rome, as Johann Burchard records, because of the presence of other rival lances in Paris (the point that had been separated from the lance), Nuremberg (see "Vienna lance"), and

Armenia (see “Echmiadzin lance”). In the mid-18th century, Benedict XIV states that he obtained from Paris an exact drawing of the point of the lance, and that in comparing it with the larger relic in St. Peter’s, he was satisfied that the two had originally formed one blade. This relic has never since left Rome, where it is preserved under the dome of Saint Peter’s Basilica, although the Church makes no claim as to its authenticity.

Echmiadzin Lance

A Holy Lance (in Armenian Geghard) is now conserved in Ejmiadzin, the religious capital of Armenia. The first source that mentions it is a text “Holy Relics of Our Lord Jesus Christ”, in a thirteenth century Armenian manuscript. According to this text, the spear which pierced Jesus was to have been brought to Armenia by the apostle Thaddeus. The manuscript does not specify precisely where it is kept, but the Holy Lance gives a description that exactly matches the lance, the monastery gate, since the thirteenth century precisely, the name of Geghardavank (Monastery of the Holy Lance).

In 1655, the French traveller Jean-Baptiste Tavernier was the first Westerner to see this relic in Armenia. In 1805, the Russians took the monastery and the relic was moved to Tchitchanov Geghard Tbilisi (Georgia). It was later returned to Armenia at Ejmiadzin, where it is always visible to the museum Manougian, enshrined in a reliquary of the seventeenth century.

This Ejmiadzin Lance has never been a weapon. Rather, it is the point of a sigillum, perhaps Byzantine, with a diamond-shaped iron openwork Greek cross. Is this the Holy Lance of Antioch discovered by Pierre Barthelemy? That is a certain assumption: the relic of the Crusaders lost chronicles a century before the Geghard appears in Armenian sources.

Vienna Lance (Hofburg Spear)

The Holy Roman Emperors had a lance of their own, attested from the time of Otto I (912-973). In 1000, Otto III gave Boleslaw I of Poland a replica of the Lance at the Congress of Gniezno. In 1084 Henry IV had a silver band with the inscription “Nail of Our Lord” added to it. This was based on the belief that this was the lance of Constantine the Great which enshrined a nail used for the Crucifixion. In 1273, it was first used in the coronation ceremony. Around 1350, Charles IV had a golden sleeve put over the silver one, inscribed "Lancea et clavus Domini" (Lance and nail of the Lord). In 1424, Sigismund had a collection of relics, including the lance, moved from his capital in Prague to his birth place, Nuremberg, and decreed them to be kept there forever. This collection was called the Reichskleinodien or Imperial Regalia.

When the French Revolutionary army approached Nuremberg in the spring of 1796, the city councillors decided to remove the Reichskleinodien to Vienna for safekeeping. The collection was entrusted to one "Baron von Hügel", who promised to return the objects as soon as peace had been restored and the safety of the collection assured. However, the Holy Roman Empire was disbanded in 1806 and the Reichskleinodien remained in the keeping of the Habsburgs. When the city councillors asked for the Reichskleinodien back, they were refused. As part of the imperial regalia, it was kept in the Imperial Treasury Schatzkammer (Vienna) and was known as the lance of Saint Maurice.

During the Anschluss, when Austria was annexed to Germany, the Reichskleinodien were returned to Nuremberg and afterwards hidden. They were found by invading U.S. troops and returned to Austria by American General George S. Patton after World War II.

Dr. Robert Feather, an English metallurgist and technical engineering writer, tested the lance for a documentary in January 2003. He was given unprecedented permission not only to examine the lance in a laboratory environment, but was allowed to remove the delicate bands of gold and silver that hold it together. In the opinion of Feather and other academic experts, the likeliest date of the spearhead is the 7th century A.D. – only slightly earlier than the Museum's own estimate. However, Dr. Feather stated in the same documentary that an iron pin – long claimed to be a nail from the crucifixion, hammered into the blade and set off by tiny brass crosses – is "consistent" in length and shape with a 1st century A.D. Roman nail. According to Paul the Deacon, the Lombard royal line bore the name of the Gungingi, which Karl Hauck and Stefano Gasparri maintain identified them with the name of Odin's lance, Gungnir (a sign that they probably claimed descent from Odin, as did most of the Germanic royal lines)

Paul the Deacon notes that the inauguration rite of a Lombard king consisted essentially of his grasping of a sacred/royal lance. Milan, which had been the capital of the Western Roman Empire in the time of Constantine, was the capital of the Lombard kings Perctarit and his son Cunipert, who became Catholic Christians in the 7th century. Thus, it seems possible that the iron point of the Lombardic royal lance might have been recast in the 7th century in order to enshrine one of the 1st century Roman nails that St. Helena was reputed to have found at Calvary and brought to Milan, thus giving a new Christian sacred aura to the old pagan royal lance. If Charlemagne's inauguration as the King of the Lombards in 774 had likewise included his grasping of this now-Christianized sacred or royal lance, this would explain how it would have eventually become the oldest item in the German imperial regalia. The Iron Crown of Lombardy (dated to the 8th century), which eventually became the primary symbol of Lombardic kingship, takes its name from the tradition that it contains one of the holy nails. Gregory of Tours in his Libri Historiarum VII, 33, states that in 585 the Merovingian king Guntram designated his nephew Childebert II his heir by handing him his lance, it is possible that a royal lance was a symbol of kingship among the Merovingian kings and that a nail from Calvary was in the 7th century incorporated into this royal lance and thus eventually would have come into the German imperial regalia.

Other Lances

Another lance has been preserved at Krakow, Poland, since at least the 13th century. However, German records indicate that it was a copy of the Vienna Lance. Emperor Henry II had it made with a small sliver of the original lance. Another copy was given to the Hungarian king at the same time.

The story told by William of Malmesbury of the giving of the Holy Lance to King Athelstan of England by Hugh Capet seems to be due to a misconception.

Modern Legends

Richard Wagner

In his opera *Parsifal,* Richard Wagner identifies the Holy Spear with two items that appear in Wolfram von Eschenbach's medieval poem

Parzival, a bleeding spear in the Castle of the Grail and the spear that has wounded the Fisher King. The opera's plot concerns the consequences of the spear's loss by the Knights of the Grail and its recovery by Parsifal. Having decided that the blood on the Spear was that of the wounded Saviour – Christ is never named in the opera – Wagner has the blood manifest itself in the Grail rather than on the spearhead.

Trevor Ravenscroft

The "Spear of Destiny" is a name given to the Holy Lance in various accounts that attribute mystical powers to it. Many of these have originated in recent times, and several popular New Age and conspiracy theory books have popularised the legend of the Spear.

Trevor Ravenscroft's 1973 book, *The Spear of Destiny* (as well as a later book, *The Mark of the Beast*), claims that Adolf Hitler started World War II in order to capture the spear, with which he was obsessed. At the end of the war, the spear came into the hands of U.S. General George Patton. According to legend, losing the spear would result in death, and that was fulfilled when Hitler committed suicide.

Ravenscroft repeatedly attempted to define the mysterious "powers" that the legend says the spear serves. He found it to be a hostile and evil spirit, which he sometimes referred to as the Antichrist, though that is open to interpretation. He never actually referred to the spear as spiritually controlled, but rather as intertwined with all of mankind's ambitions.

Howard Buechner

Dr. Howard A. Buechner, M.D., professor of medicine at Tulane and then Louisiana State University, wrote two books on the spear. Buechner was a retired colonel with the U.S. Army who served in World War II and had written a book about the Dachau massacre. He claims that he was contacted by a former U-boat submariner, the pseudonymous "Capt. Wilhelm Bernhart," who claimed the spear currently on display in Vienna is a fake. "Bernhart" said the real spear was sent by Hitler to Antarctica along with other Nazi treasures, under the command of Col. Maximilian Hartmann. In 1979, Hartmann allegedly recovered the treasures. Bernhart presented Buechner with the log from this expedition as well as pictures of the objects recovered, claiming that after the Spear of Destiny was recovered, it was hidden somewhere in Europe by a Nazi secret society. After contacting most of the members of the alleged expedition and others involved, including Hitler Youth Leader Artur Axmann, Buechner became convinced the claims were true.

Otto Rahn – Seeker of the Grail

Otto Wilhelm Rahn (February 18, 1904 – March 13, 1939) was a German medievalist and a Obersturmführer (First Lieutenant) of the SS, born in Michelstadt, Germany.

Speculation still swirls around Otto Rahn and his research. From an early age, he became interested in the legends of Parsifal, Holy Grail, Lohengrin, and the Nibelungenlied. While attending the University of Giessen he was inspired by his Professor, the Baron von Gall, to study the Albigensian (Catharism) movement, and the massacre that occurred at Montségur. Rahn is quoted as saying, "It was a subject that completely captivated me."

Work

In 1931, he travelled to the Pyrenees region of southern France where he conducted most of his research. Aided by the French mystic and historian Antonin Gadal, Rahn argued that there was a direct link between Wolfram Von Eschenbach's Parzival and the Cathar Grail mystery. He believed that the Cathars held the answer to this sacred mystery and that the keys to their secrets lay somewhere beneath the mountain pog where the fortress of Montségur remains, the last Cathar fortress to fall during the Albigensian Crusade.

Otto Rahn with his wife and child

Rahn believed it was possible to trace the Cathars, who guarded the Holy Grail in their castle at Montsegur, back to Druids who converted to Gnostic Manichaeism. The Druids in Britain were forerunners of the Celtic Christian Church. He saw that the culture of the medieval Cathar stronghold of Languedoc bore strong a resemblance to the ancient Druids. Their priests were akin to the Cathar Parfaits. The Cathar secret wisdom being preserved by the later Troubadours, the travelling poets and singers of the medieval courts of France – M. Sabeheddin (Countermedia).

Rahn's SS Service and Death

Rahn wrote two books linking Montségur and Cathars with the Holy Grail: *Kreuzzug gegen den Gral* (Crusade Against the Grail) in 1933 and *Luzifers Hofgesind* (Lucifer's Court) in 1937. After the publication of his first book, Rahn's work came to the attention of Heinrich Himmler, the head of the SS, who was fascinated by the occult and had already initiated research in the south of France.

Rahn joined his staff as a junior non-commissioned officer and became a full member of the SS in 1936. Journeys for his second book led Rahn to places in Germany, France, Italy and Iceland.

Openly homosexual, he was assigned guard duty at the Dachau concentration camp in 1937 as punishment for a drunken homosexual scrape. He resigned from the SS in 1939.

On March 13, 1939 nearly on the anniversary of the fall of Montségur, Rahn was found frozen to death on a mountainside near Söll (Kufstein, Tyrol) in Austria. His death was officially ruled a suicide.

Rahn in Popular Culture

Rahn has been described as the inspiration behind the Indiana Jones movie *Raiders of the Lost Ark*, although neither George Lucas nor Steven Spielberg has ever mentioned anything about his having inspired the film.

Rahn has been the object of many rumours and strange stories, including that his death had been faked, although all such speculation has failed to be substantiated. He features as a character in the 2008 novel *The Judas Apocalypse* by Dan McNeil. In the novel, Rahn helps a fellow German archaeologist search for the lost treasure of the

Cathars. He also figures in the "Berlin Noir" novel *The Pale Criminal* by Philip Kerr and *Blood Lance* by Craig Smith. In the Italian comic book *Martin Mystère*, Rahn fakes his death and joins the U.S. secret service "Elsewhere".

Richard Stanley, cult director of such films as *Hardware* and *Dust Devil*, also made a documentary about Rahn and his fixation on the Holy Grail called *The Secret Glory* in 2001.